survival kit

for substitute

VITA PAVLICH and ELEANOR ROSENAST
Elementary School Substitutes
Los Angeles City Schools

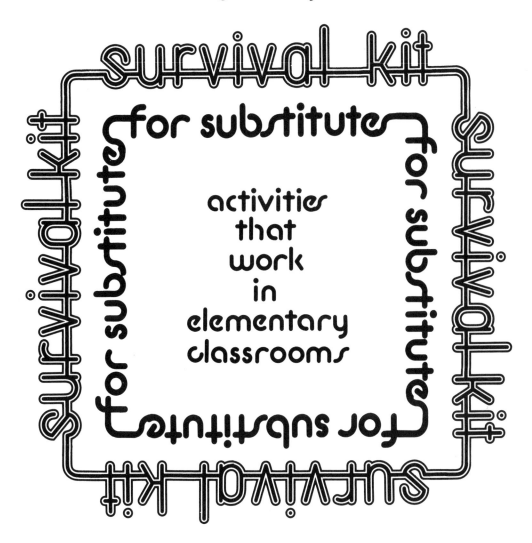

survival kit
for substitutes

activities
that
work
in
elementary
classrooms

CITATION PRESS NEW YORK 1974

Library of Congress Catalog Card Number: 73-89775
International Standard Book Number: 0-590-0957-7
Cover design by Lucy Bitzer

Published by Citation Press, Library and Trade Division,
Scholastic Magazines, Inc.
Editorial Office: 50 West 44th Street, New York, New York 10036.
Printed in the U.S.A.

5   6   7   8   81   80   79   78

For Al Cullum

contents

Art with Limited Materials   77

survival kit

for substitute

Foreword

This book is intended to be a source of ideas and activities for substitute teachers of elementary grades. The ideas come from our own teaching experiences as well as those of other teachers.

We have tried to write up the activities as concisely as possible, feeling that the essence of this book is *action*. For that reason we deliberately refrained from discussing the educational rationale of each activity. Nevertheless, each idea is sound—to develop or reinforce skills, spur the imagination, or encourage problem-solving.

Feel confident that these ideas are workable for large city school classes—this is where they've been used.

V. P.

E. R.

Keys to survival and success

A substitute teacher *can* be something more than a baby-sitter. The baby-sitting sub becomes a policeman who turns into a witch!

The frustrating experiences of many substitutes reveal how children really feel about school restrictions and the adults who impose them. A sub is often the perfect scapegoat for these feelings because of her temporary status. She is on very shaky ground if she sees herself in the authoritative position of the regular teacher.

As a substitute your situation is an uneasy one because you are in strange territory. You face a new work situation each day—new children to work with and a new administrator to observe your work. Usually this means you are expected to "control" a class. You feel the tension of trying to show that you can—to both the students and the administrator.

When a substitute appears, the children see the day as a break in their regular schedule. The key to survival (and success) is to take advantage of this feeling and to provide activities that are a refreshing break in the day-to-day routine.

Here are some steps you can take to make the new territory familiar and less threatening.

☐ Arrive at school early.

☐ Check the storeroom to see what is available.

☐ Examine the room. Open all closets, cupboards, and drawers. Know what is in the room. The available materials will help you to select some of your activities for the day.

☐ Check to see doors are unlocked so that children can enter freely. A locked door and a harassed teacher searching for the key raises tensions.

☐ Invite in one or two of the "peekers" (curious children). They can cue you in to many things—where they are in different subjects, school routines, and the like.

☐ Set aside a few minutes to learn a few names from the attendance list, maybe five. When the children come in, call those names immediately and ask their owners to do small jobs. They will be surprised and pleased that you know their names. It helps to establish a good rapport. The more names you can quickly connect with faces, the better rapport you can build.

☐ Allow the class to conduct the opening exercises in their accustomed way, i. e., flag salute, attendance, money collections, monitors' jobs, and so forth.

A quick, good first impression is essential since you don't have a past relationship to build on. Your initial activity must be intriguing and capture the children's attention.

Keep your talk and explanations brief and simple. If you

have a good idea, but it needs a long explanation, forget it! It's probably a measurable phenomenon that the more a teacher talks, the less the children listen.

Distribute materials in an organized way. This helps to keep a serene atmosphere. Use a cafeteria-style method in which children help themselves for clumsy or spillable items. Other things can be passed around easily.

If you give an assignment that requires checking, have the children do the checking themselves. They really do learn more that way. Besides, it has obvious teacher advantages.

Have the children work with partners or in teams as often as possible. They enjoy it. Also, if what you're introducing is new and unusual, working with someone else is more comfortable for them.

A change of pace in the schedule is necessary. After a sedentary activity, do something involving more movement. For example, if you do creative writing, follow it with an art or drama activity. When you sense that a change is needed (and unmistakable signs will tell you), don't hesitate to shorten the ongoing activity.

Be over-prepared. Have in mind many kinds of activities to do. Think about all the suggestions in this book frequently, so they'll be at your fingertips.

Prepare your own basic kit of materials that are not readily available in most classrooms. The materials should be multi-purpose and adaptable for use at different grade levels. Weigh the materials you choose against the time and complexity of the activity. It doesn't pay to drag along a heavy book for a ten-minute presentation.

To create a dramatic initial impression on the children, bring your materials in a colorful or exciting-looking carrier. For example, a suitcase decorated in an unusual way, a fancy shopping bag, or, if you're courageous, a crazy duffle bag.

At the end of the day leave the teacher a resume of what the class did. If you can't be positive, be noncommital.

Try to leave the room in good order.

And finally, try to stay out of a corner, but if you are trapped (figuratively, of course) and a threat is wrenched out of you, make it a vague one.

Keep your problems in the classroom. You're there for one day, so it's best to handle any difficulties yourself.

Children, like all people, enjoy feeling they are special. You'll find them very receptive if you approach them with the idea that you want them to experiment with new activities and that you want their participation and evaluation. Beginning the day with a new and different activity is an excellent way to build a harmonious relationship with them.

"Openers" are most effective if you can introduce them with minimum talking or explaining. The object is to let the children know something different is happening by what they can *see*.

CODES

Put a coded message on the board *before the children come in the room.* It should include your name. For example, a simple code is A is 1, B is 2, C is 3, and so on.

Give time for the children to figure it out. Then have them

write their own name in the same code. They might then write their favorite animal, food, color, sport, or TV program. Have them exchange papers and decipher each other's codes. They can share their findings with the class.

If interest is still high, go on to discuss other codes. For example, Z is 1, Y is 2, X is 3, and so on.

For real cryptologists, try this one:

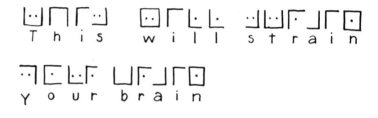

a	b	c
d	e	f
g	h	i

J.	k.	l.
m.	n.	o.
p.	q.	r.

s..	t..	u..
v..	w..	x..
y..	z..	

SUPERSTITION ACTIVITIES

As a way of introducing these activities bring a bag of fortune cookies to school with you; put one cookie on each desk before the children come in. On the board write a message such as: "Resist temptation . . . . until 9:17 a.m."

Conduct the usual daily business and then at the appointed time ask everyone to break open his cookie and read his fortune. The children will be anxious to read their fortunes to each other, so allow time for that. Afterwards, discuss with them what the word "fortune" suggests, such as the superstitions of various peoples and their magical and occult practices.

Make a list on the board of all superstitions the children can think of. They might illustrate them or dramatize them in teams. Creating a mural on superstitions would also be exciting.

Numerology

Explain what numerology is and have the children figure out their primary number for the day and what it signifies.

According to numerologists, every number has a certain power. They use a simplified alphabetical and numerical code worked out by the ancient Greeks.

Numbers one to nine are primary numbers—all other numbers are reduced to these nine.

The most popular method used to reduce all numbers to the primary 9 is to add the figures of the number—for example, 236 is $2 + 3 + 6 = 11$. Next add the two digits in 11; $1 + 1 = 2$. Two then is the symbol for 236.

Another example is $69,431 - 6 + 9 + 4 + 3 + 1 = 23$; $2 + 3 = 5$.

According to numerologists there are good days and bad days, depending on one's number for the day. One can decide what actions should be done and not done on certain days. What will your day be like today? What do your numbers tell you?

To find your primary number for the day, follow this formula:

Birth Number
e.g., July 2, 1961: 7 (seventh month) $+ 2 + 1 + 9 + 6 + 1 = 26$; $2 + 6 = 8$
8 is your birth number

Name Number
A n n a P a v l i c h
$1 + 5 + 5 + 1 + 7 + 1 + 4 + 3 + 9 + 3 + 8 = 47$;
$4 + 7 = 11$; $1 + 1 = 2$
2 is your name number.

The following chart may be used to determine a name number:

1	2	3	4	5	6	7	8	9
A	B	C	D	E	F	G	H	I
J	K	L	M	N	O	P	Q	R
S	T	U	V	W	X	Y	Z	

Z is the twenty-sixth letter of the alphabet. Its symbol becomes 8 when the two digits 2 and 6 are added.

The other letters are given numerical equivalents in the same way. J is the tenth letter of the alphabet. The digits 1 and 0 are added. They equal 1, so J is placed in the 1 column.

Number of the Day
e. g., September 9, 1971.
Use the above chart to find out the value of each letter in the name of the month.
S   e   p   t   e   m   b   e   r   9
$1 + 5 + 7 + 2 + 5 + 4 + 2 + 5 + 9 + 9 + 1 + 9 + 7 + 1 = 67; 6 + 7 = 13; 1 + 3 = 4$

Add the totals of composite numbers (birth number, name number, and number of day): $8 + 2 + 4 = 14; 1 + 4 = 5$. This is your primary number for the day. Check the table of numbers to see what your number tells you.

Table of Numbers

1. A day for action. Time to attack any problem that needs to be taken care of immediately. A good time to start something new or to ask advice. Nothing complicated should be begun on this day.

2. A day to plan, to consider problems rather than acting on them right away. This day may begin well and end badly or begin badly and end well. Many contrasts — a day to take it easy.

3. Much can be done today, many projects can be started

with help from others. A good day for meeting people, travel, and fun.

4. A day to finish up small practical jobs—things that should have been done. Fun things won't work out too well on this day.

5. A day for the unexpected—excitement and adventure. Take risks, but know that the goal is worth the chances you're taking.

6. A day for comfort and good will. No conflict today. Not a time for quick actions, but rather a time for family and social affairs. Not a time to take risks.

7. A day for study, invention, or art projects. A time for planning and thinking things out. You can ask advice. A good day to play your hunches. A lucky day for you.

8. A day to undertake big and important things. Complicated matters can be dealt with today.

9. Aim for big achievements. This is the day to announce big plans. It promises good work in artistic fields.

Astrology

Ask the class what they know about astrology. List the astrological time periods on the board, leaving room for children's names. Then have each child list his name under the appropriate period.

Pass out a ditto or read the characteristics of each zodiac sign. The class will obviously want to discuss them, but if you feel they need a change in tempo, have them write down their impressions, or whether they agree or disagree. Another way of handling a discussion would be to have all children under the same sign come up to the front and evaluate themselves in terms of the astrological characteristics. You may need to explain some of them a little more fully.

March 21–April 19: Aries the Ram
Creative person
Active and ambitious nature
Begins projects but is easily diverted
Angers quickly but calms down easily
Good sense of humor
Can get others to work with them on new projects but
often quits before finished
Loyal, will fight for what they think right
Natural leaders, eager to lead the way
Good salesmen, actors, lawyers, and statesmen
Enjoys music

April 20–May 19: Taurus the Bull
Strong and stubborn
Led by emotion rather than reason
Excellent memory
Plans ahead and finishes projects
Well-liked, becomes a good friend, generous, shares his
money
Likes games, sports, music, drama
Usually trustworthy and faithful, but can get furious
Do well as engineers, builders, good in chemistry, some
famous explorers

May 20–June 20: Gemini the Twins
Easily adapts to change
Figures things out and acts quickly
Imaginative, generous, and affectionate
Likes change, becomes easily dissatisfied
Popular
Learns new things quickly, clever, and witty
Feels sure of himself, but tends to scatter his energy rather
than focus it
Good business person, does well in advertising and pub-
lishing and as television writers and artists

June 21–July 22: Cancer the Crab

Home-loving, enjoys family life, but also likes to travel and have adventure

Enjoys the past or the old ways of doing things

Sensitive, but often doesn't show it

Feelings hurt by criticism, crawls into his shell, moody

Loyal to family and friends

Imaginative, tends to be jealous

Strong determination

Does well in business as manufacturers and merchants, also good teachers, librarians, scientists, and musicians

July 23–August 21: Leo the Lion

Powerful personality, born leaders, ambitious, impulsive

Generous and brave

Likes activity, outdoors, and sun

Can become lazy

Stands up for friends and family, criticizes people who disagree with them

Easily flattered

Good doctors and nurses, famous actors, real estate developers

August 22–September 22: Virgo the Virgin

Capable people but difficult personalities

Curious minds, really look into things, excellent memories

Finds fault with people and projects

Fearful of accidents, illness, and financial problems

Doesn't like to think of unhappy things

Quick minds, alert, and hard working

Good teachers, writers, editors, lawyers

September 23–October 22: Libra the Scales
Tries to make friends, sympathetic, helpful to friends or
strangers
Stands up for underdog
Generous and expects that quality in others
Likes amusements and excitement
Fond of music
Original in ideas, needs to learn to accept criticism
Often are inventors, good in research
Make good actors, musicians, and singers

October 23–November 21: Scorpio the Scorpion
Fearless nature, great self-control, and confidence
Quiet people but know what's going on
Strong when roused to action
Satisfied with self
Can become domineering
Ability to overcome problems
Strong in business, great doctors

November 22–December 21: Sagittarius the Bowman
Cheerful, happy dispositions
Very active and capable, works very hard to get things done
Helps charitable causes
Minds own business
Outspoken and sometimes offends in that way
Likes to travel
Good prospectors, air pilots, sea captains, and scientists

December 22–January 21: Capricorn the Goat
Deep thinkers, have gloomy moods
Good organizers
Loves solitude
Criticism worries them, may even make them stop trying
Desires success

Good managers in business and finance, writers, teachers, and lawyers

January 21–February 19: Aquarius the Water Carrier
Many try to help humanity (active in social causes)
Does things in a quiet way
Good memories
Friendly and popular but also likes to be alone
Can curb temper
May tend to be lazy; self-reliant and confident
Good bargainers; do well in law and politics and as scientists and inventors

February 20–March 20: Pisces the Fish
Modest, unselfish
Often doubts own ability and fears future
Sincere and trustworthy but often fooled by others
Are appreciated by their friends
Calm, devoted to friends
Does well in government jobs, science and engineering
Interested in nature

The children can also do an art activity based on their zodiac sign. The crayon scratch technique can produce exciting results. Cover a paper (a heavy kind, if possible) with layers of colorful crayon. Then cover the entire surface with heavy black crayon. (You'll need to bring extra black crayons with you.) Scratch out a design with a pin, paperclip, or other sharp instrument.

ART ACTIVITIES

Art activities make wonderful openers because the children are always responsive. The art chapter has many ideas that are perfect for openers, for example, murals, graph paper designs, name designs, paper construction, or miniatures.

GUESSING GAMES

Make it your business to have a full purse with some unusual items in it. Divide the class in half. Hold up your purse and tell the teams to list everything they think is in it. At a given time they stop, and you then take out each item as they check it off their lists. You might score ten points for a correct guess and minus five for a wrong guess. For primary children do this without scoring.

Also for primary grades, have some tiny object in a small box. Tell the children you want them to guess what's in the box, but you'll give them some hints. Using primary reading vocabulary, write one hint at a time on the board until interest wanes or they guess the object.

MAKING BUTTER

The way to a primary child's heart is through his stomach. Also, many children have no idea how butter is made.

Bring with you a quart-size jar with a tight lid, a half pint of whipping cream, a knife, and a box of crackers.

Using primary reading vocabulary, write the directions for making the butter on the board. The class reads them together.

1. Put the cream in the jar.
2. Put the cover on the jar.
3. Shake the jar up and down.
4. Each boy shakes the jar 15 times.
5. Each girl shakes the jar 15 times.
6. Here comes the butter.

As each child shakes the jar, the rest of the class helps him count. Eat the finished butter and crackers or save for later, depending on the temper of the group.

If you're a courageous substitute, try this in the upper grades upgrading the vocabulary of the directions.

HAND PUPPETS

Before the children come in, think of several common names. Using a hand puppet ask, "Is there a Mary in the room?" If she answers, have a short conversation with her. "Do you have a pet?" "What sports do you enjoy?" and the like. Then ask who would like to be the puppet and ask questions.

Another primary grade opener is to have the children clap a rhythm of their names based on the number of syllables. Or ask a child to repeat his name and move with the sound of it. Then have the entire group do the movement.

PROPS

You need to be uninhibited, courageous, and have a dramatic flair for these activities. Props create excitement and help break down the image of a stiff school-teacher. A teacher who feels comfortable with children's laughter will be able to channel their excitement into a creative experience. The very fact of the teacher bringing pleasure will establish rapport with the class.

Wear a pair of long gloves to school. Keep them on as you attend to the morning routines. Dramatize them by making exaggerated movements. Then slowly take them off and place them on the desk trying to keep the shape of your hand. Ask the children, "Where have these gloves been?" Try to get responses that are imaginative and fanciful. When you ask them to write they'll feel freer.

You can do a similar thing with an unusual hat. Talk about "Who has worn this hat?"

Another prop could be an umbrella that you keep open, use as a parasol, or twirl as you walk around the room.

The most popular prop you can bring is a musical instrument to play to the children.

MATERIALS NOT USUALLY FOUND IN CLASSROOMS

SUPERSTITION ACTIVITIES
Fortune cookies.
Dittos or chart of information on characteristics of primary numbers for numerology.
Dittos or chart of information on zodiac signs

ART ACTIVITIES
Roll of kraft paper.
Pad of graph paper.
Name designs (see art chapter for instructions).

GUESSING GAMES
Purse with unusual items.
Small box with tiny object.

MAKING BUTTER
A quart jar with lid.
½-pint whipping cream, knife, and crackers.

PROPS
Hand puppet, pair of gloves, unusual hat, or musical instrument.

This reading chapter is divided into two parts. The first can be used when you prefer not to follow the teacher's reading plan. The second can be used when you are following the teacher's routine and need only a little bit extra to augment it. However, it is often difficult and time-consuming for a substitute on a one-day assignment to figure out the regular teacher's reading plan.

Younger children become easily confused when their routine is changed. Even if the sub does attempt to follow established procedures, the result is usually different, and thus children will easily accept and enjoy a completely new approach.

READING ON YOUR OWN — PRIMARY GRADES

Alphabet Activities

Use the letters of the alphabet as a basis for a design. Draw very large block letters on the blackboard. Have the children write words beginning with that letter within the drawing of the block letter. The fun of this activity is to squeeze as many words as possible into the block letter. They can begin with words they know and then use books to find more. As a variation the children can draw their own block letters on 8½ × 11 inch paper, cut them out and do the same activity. If you wish, prepare your own block letter patterns using initial consonant sounds.

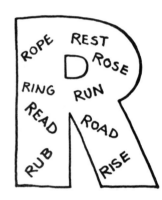

Prepare two decks of alphabet cards on 3 × 5 inch cards. One set should be in upper case and the other in lower case letters. Shuffle the cards and give out one set. The children hold the cards and arrange themselves alphabetically. Give out lower case cards to one group, upper case to another. Have children find matching partners.

Spread both sets of cards face down on the floor and play concentration. A child picks up two cards, hoping to find matching pairs. If he is unsuccessful, he replaces them face down. The other children concentrate on the location of the replaced cards so that during their own turns they have a better chance of finding matching cards. (These alphabet card games can also be played with cards having days of the week, and months or seasons of the year.)

Use the initial sound of a child's name. Have the group make up a short story repeating the sound as often as possible. For example, "David's dog digs deep down." The teacher writes the story on paper, and each child illustrates his own story. He tries to read it to a friend. An additional activity is to make a duplicate copy of the story and have each child cut out the words and match them to the first story.

Directions

Draw a left and right hand on the board. The children can come up and match their own hands.

Have the children look for identifying marks on either hand.

After some practice, have children move their hands around in the air, then call for the right or left hand to be raised. For children who continue to have trouble, make a masking tape bracelet marked right and left.

Children trace outlines of each hand on paper putting in identifying marks and labeling them right and left. They can do the same thing with their feet.

When they're familiar with their right and left hands, they can identify their right and left shoulder, eye, knee—anything to give variety and practice.

Sing the song "Looby Loo" and play the game at the same time. It's a game using right and left parts of the body. Children stand in a circle and sing or say: "You put your right hand in, You put your right hand out, You give your right hand a shake, shake, shake, and turn yourself about. You put your left hand in," and so on.

Titles

Discuss the meaning of Mr., Mrs., Miss, and Ms.

Have the children make illustrations of their family giving each member of the family his appropriate title.

Make a family book. This can include pages showing each member of the family doing his job, the pets of the family, a picture of the family car, the appearance of the house or apartment (write in address and phone number), or what they want to be when they grow up. Use the children's suggestions of what to include in the book.

Sound Families

The children create fanciful figures using sound families, such as, "an ump lump," "an ock rock," or "an am lamb." They can compose poems or stories using these family sounds and illustrate them.

Play a rhyming game with the children. The teacher gives a word. The children have to think of one word to go with the word given. For the next word given, they have to think of two rhyming words. Continue in this way increasing the number of rhyming words needed.

Nursery Rhymes

Read nursery rhymes to the children. Let the group say them along with you. Have individuals recite rhymes they know.

Dramatize the rhymes.

The children can make individual pictures of the rhymes. These can be cut out and pasted on a mural and a background colored in.

Riddles can be made up about the rhymes. For example, "Who Am I? I'm round. I had a terrible accident, and nobody could help me."

Stories and Poems

Read the children a story. Have them recreate the sequences in pictures.

Read several short poems that contain strong images and have the children illustrate them. A good collection for primary children is *Poems Children Will Sit Still For* which includes good suggestions for how to involve children in many of these poems.

The above activities can be used with limericks and nonsense verses too.

READING ON YOUR OWN—UPPER GRADES

Story Reading

Read the children a short story such as "William Tell" in *Stories to Dramatize* by Winifred Ward.

The children can then draw an illustrated map showing where the events of the story took place, write a different ending to the story, make a book jacket for the story including a blurb about it, or recreate the story in comic strip form.

Word Fill-Ins

Hand out a mimeographed paragraph in which every fifth or eighth word is omitted. Ask the children to fill in the gaps, using any word that keeps the sense of the paragraph. For example:

One summer morning, bright <u>and</u> early, the little old <u>man</u> put a geranium red <u>cap</u> upon his head, and <u>he</u> lifted his big, brown <u>pack</u> up and over his <u>shoulder.</u> Then he started down <u>the</u> forest path, for he <u>was</u> on his way to sell his caps. He had <u>not</u> gone far when he <u>saw</u> a beautiful patch <u>of</u> golden dandelions. He stopped <u>and</u> picked a long stemmed <u>one</u> and stuck it in <u>the</u> top of his cap. <u>Then</u> he took a long <u>look</u> at the sky. There <u>was</u> something about the clouds <u>that</u> told the little old <u>man</u> that it would be <u>wise</u> for him to go <u>to</u> the south for the <u>day.</u> And with his mind <u>made</u> up he was soon <u>on</u> his way again.

Have the children write their own paragraphs, leaving out words in a similar way. They exchange papers with a neighbor and complete each other's paragraphs.

Writing a Story

Read a story in a specific genre such as a fable or tall tale. Discuss its characteristic elements with the children and list them on the board. Keeping these in mind, have them try to write a story as a group and then possibly alone, if they're ready for such an activity. Here are some examples:

Cumulative Stories: "The Gingerbread Boy," "Henny-Penny," "Three Little Pigs," "Ask Mr. Bear" (a modern one). The characteristics of cumulative stories are a simple plot, story moves quickly, repetition of action and dialogue, and usually an element of surprise at the end. Although these tales are simple, don't avoid using them with older children who will be more aware of their elements.

Fairy Tales: Read a fairy tale, then list the fairy tales the children have read. List their elements. The characteristics of fairy tales are that they usually deal with royalty—king and queen, prince or princess—fairies, witches, giants, and the like. The plot usually involves enchantments and spells. The hero or heroine usually is the youngest child and they have to overcome difficulties and accomplish hard tasks to succeed. Love, bravery, and good deeds are necessary to break the spells and win the princess and half the kingdom. Good usually triumphs over evil.

Tall Tales: The characters are boastful supermen such as Paul Bunyan, Pecos Bill, or John Henry. Omit the latter if the children are not familiar with tall tales. If they are, read one to refresh their memories. Characteristics are the heroes are work heroes from a special geographic locale, they're experts in what they do, and they think big and go in for exaggeration. The tales often tell outright lies, but they're clothed in details that make them seem believable. The exaggerations are humorous.

Fables: Initiate this activity by reading a fable. Most children have read many of them but may not be familiar with the term "fable." Make a list of the fables children have read. Some examples are: "The Hare and the Tortoise," "The Lion and the Mouse," "The Fox and the Crow," and "Town Mouse and Country Mouse." Characteristics are talking animals, each of whom has a dominant trait, a short and simple plot, usually involving one significant act that points up a moral lesson, and frequently a pretentious character versus a simple one. With primary children, forget the discussion of the characteristics and just have them make up a typical fable.

Publishing

Encyclopedia: Encyclopedias can be made using themes of fairy tales, tall tales, fables, or favorite characters from books the children are reading.

Using fairy tales as an example, list with the children famous fairy tale characters such as Sleeping Beauty, Cinderella, and Jack and the Beanstalk.

Each child chooses one or more characters, illustrates them, and then writes a short sketch telling whatever he thinks is important or interesting about them, such as who they are, or what their problems are. Try to avoid making this a book report.

Children can choose partners and help each other correct spelling and punctuation. A good method is to have them read their work aloud to each other so they can hear where sentences end. The substitute teacher circulates to help out where needed. After corrections, the work should be rewritten with careful attention to handwriting. The children will be eager to do their best work.

An encyclopedia is organized alphabetically, so the teacher can call out for characters beginning with A, B, C, and so on. A book cover can be made of large colored paper, and it can be illustrated. The contributors should be listed alphabetically at the beginning. A table of contents can be made too. This project, with its varied jobs, involves all the children in the class.

It is also very exciting to publish an "encyclopedia" on large pieces of butcher paper. Illustrations can be glued on and the text written underneath with a felt pen.

Dictionary: The teacher can say, "Let's make our own dictionary. I'll give a word and you give me a definition. Don't use the word in the definition." After the teacher gives a few words, the children can offer words of their own to be defined by the class.

The children can pair up with partners and decide on a word they would like the class to define. Each member of the class writes a definition, which is then handed to the team that gave the word. (The word and its editors can be listed on the board.) Every child writes a definition for every word given.

The editors choose four or five of the best definitions. They edit for punctuation and spelling. They rewrite the word and its definitions, paying attention to handwriting. Since every child is an editor, everyone gets the experience.

Since a dictionary is organized alphabetically, the teacher calls for all words beginning with A, then B, and so on. A book cover can be made for the collected definitions. The dictionary can be published on large pieces of butcher paper.

If the compilation is put together on butcher paper and there are several words on a page, guide words can be chosen for the top of each page. This is one of those long, involving projects that can cover many subject areas in a creative and exciting way.

In primary grades a dictionary project may be done orally. After the words are defined together, the class may divide into two groups. One group works with the teacher, who writes the word definitions given by the children; the children in the other group illustrate their own words. Then the groups switch. The teacher calls for the words alphabetically, and the illustrated papers are put in a book.

Riddle Book: Have the class tell riddles they know. Discuss with the children how riddles are written. They should be aware that clues have a double meaning. Then have the children write and illustrate their own riddles. The illustration should be done on separate pieces of paper. Children can share their projects with each other and work together as partners. Collate the papers in a book and make a cover.

As a variation each child or set of partners can make their own riddle book.

Illustrating Poetry

Using May H. Arbuthnot's *Anthology of Children's Literature* or any other collection, read a ballad, discuss it, and have some of the children draw their conceptions of it on paper while others work at the board.

Read limericks and let the children illustrate them.

Read nonsense rhymes and illustrate them.

Do the same with any other type of poem that contains clear, vivid images.

List Making

This is a good organizational exercise for consolidating information on a specific topic. Children enjoy the challenge of finding how many things they can think of in a particular category. A long list of examples in a specific subject makes that topic understandable. For example:

Superstitions: Discuss with the children the meaning of superstitions. Give some examples such as breaking a mirror is bad luck, walking under a ladder is bad luck, wishing on the first star, if your nose itches someone is talking about you, or if you drop a fork company is coming.

Children, individually, or with a partner, can compile a list of as many superstitions as they can think of. The list can then be used as the basis for a game of charades in which they dramatize the superstitions without words and the others try to guess them. The list of superstitions can also be illustrated.

Twin words: Children can be made aware of the multiple meanings of words. Use the term "twin words" and give some examples, such as date (fruit - calendar), match, and bark. Alone or with partners they compile as long a list of twin words as they can. The lists can be shared or illustrated to show the difference in meaning.

As a variation children can list homonyms, pairs of synonyms, or pairs of antonyms. They can refer to books for ideas.

Cliches: Discuss with the children the meaning of "cliche." Give examples such as "deep as the ocean," "quiet as a mouse," "hard as a rock," or "slow as a turtle."

Working in teams, they can create their own lists. The lists may be shared. Then ask the children to try to be more inventive. Choose one of the cliches, and ask someone to change the image. For example, "deep as the ocean" could be "deep as . . . ."

Idiomatic Expressions: Begin this lesson by reading *Amelia Bedelia* by Peggy Parish. This story is about a housekeeper who doesn't understand idioms and takes every direction literally. For example, the instruction to dust the furniture she interprets to dust the furniture with dusting powder. The story illustrates the idea of idiomatic expressions. Compile a list with the children, for example, "cut it out," and "make the bed." The idioms can be dramatized to show their literal meanings.

Other Kinds of Lists:

☐ First names
☐ Second names
☐ Movie stars
☐ TV programs
☐ Kinds of desserts
☐ Things that are red, brown, smooth, wet, and the like
☐ Night sounds, morning sounds
☐ Cars

☐ Things that come in twos (twins, gloves, shoes)
☐ Things that come in threes (triplets, triangles)

Making the Most of a Bilingual Class

Ask the children if anyone knows another language besides English. If a child volunteers, ask him to say one word. He is the expert. Ask the group to guess the meaning. Ask for a volunteer who doesn't know the language to pronounce the word. Check with the expert on proper pronunciation. Continue in this way until interest wanes, then put on the board the English equivalents. See how many foreign words the children can remember.

Vocabulary Development

Divide the class into three groups. Have each group work together looking in the dictionary to find five words for which they can demonstrate the meanings. You might start them off by demonstrating one yourself, for example, "parched." It's exciting as each team tries to work quietly together so the other teams don't hear their words.

A child from one team writes a word on the board and pronounces it. Then he demonstrates its meaning by actions, noises, or dialogue, that will clarify the meaning. The other groups try to guess the definition.

When all the groups are finished there will be three lists of words on the board. See how many meanings the children remember. You'll be surprised to see how many they know.

Rhyming Words

Divide the class into teams, and list their names on the board.

For the first round, the teacher gives a word such as "tool." Each team decides on and writes down one rhyming word. At a signal pencils go down. The teacher asks each team for its word. If it is correct, that team gets one point.

Next round, the teacher gives another word. Teams have to come up with two rhyming words. If they do, they get two points. Continue in this way, each time increasing the number of rhyming words needed and the number of points given.

Creative Writing

Here are some topics that can spark interest:

☐ Have an old glove available, and ask the class to write about "Who has worn this glove?"

☐ Pass around an interesting medallion. Suggest that it has magical powers. After examining it, let them write about it.

☐ Take off your shoe and ask, "Where has this shoe been?"

☐ Pet peeves.

☐ Autobiography of an insect. Describe the world through the eyes of an insect or an animal.

☐ My secret hideaway, imaginary or real.

☐ How colors affect me. Use the book *Hailstones and Halibut Bones* by Mary O'Neill as a starter.

☐ Tongue twisters, for example, Peter Piper picked a peck of pickled peppers . . . and she sells sea shells at the sea shore . . .

☐ Letter writing. The children can write Dear Abby letters. The letters are exchanged and each child becomes Abby and answers a letter.

☐ Choose a famous living person (sports, TV, movies, or authors,) and write a letter to him or her.

☐ A print or good magazine picture often stimulates story writing.

☐ Writing stories for younger children. Discuss with children the elements of lower grade reading material, that is limited vocabulary, much repetition, few words on a page, and illustrations to clarify the text. Have them write a story they think is suitable for primary grades.

Children should read them to each other and evaluate on the basis of the above elements.

☐ Poetry with a pattern such as cinquain. The pattern of this type of poem is quick to explain, easy for the children to understand and do, and the results are satisfying. The pattern is: first line—one word, second line—two words, third line—three words, fourth line—four words, fifth line—one word punch line. For example,

> Lighthouse
> Bright light
> Warns of danger
> Stands lonely in fog
> Beware!

☐ Read several limericks just for enjoyment using May H. Arbuthnot's *Anthology of Children's Literature* or *The Complete Nonesense of Edward Lear*. Then read a limerick and have the children label rhyming words:

> There was an old man with a nose, (A)
> Who said, "If you choose to suppose, (A)
> That my nose is too long, (B)
> You are certainly wrong," (B)
> That remarkable man with a nose. (A)

Read several limericks, noting the pattern each time, until the children master it. Then have them write their own, illustrate them, and share them with the class.

Spelling

Spelling T: Choose captains who then divide the class into two teams. As a sub you don't know the spelling strength in the group. For the game to be fun, the teams should be equal in ability. The children will see to that.

Line up behind a starting point facing the chalkboard.

The teacher draws a T on the board and puts a word on the crossline.

At a signal the first person in each line goes up to the board and writes a word beginning with the last letter of the teacher's word. They then go to their seats.

The next person in each team writes a word beginning with the last letter of the previous word written by their team member. They sit down. This continues until both teams are seated.

The team finishing first gets five points. Words spelled correctly get one point; misspelled words minus one point. If a word has more than four letters, score a point for each letter after the fourth.

After playing the game once, stop and talk about using prefixes and suffixes as ways of extending the length of words. Use the lists on the board from the game to demonstrate.

Play the game a second time. You'll see the difference.

Lists: The teacher calls out a letter. The children write as many words as they can think of in one minute that begins with that letter. Score one point for each correctly spelled word. For variations call out other categories such as names, words ending in *ed, ing,* proper nouns, descriptive words, or blends such as *bl* or *st.* Points are gained by long lists spelled correctly.

Hangman: Draw a gallows. Write a word on the board, filling in the first and last letters only: h___e (house). With each wrong letter guessed add a part of the body to the figure hanging on the gallows.

Children continue guessing the missing letters until a complete figure is hanging from the gallows or they have figured out the word.

Variation on Hangman: In this one the teacher competes against the class. She places a short sentence on the board, putting dashes in place of the letters and separating words by diagonal lines. For example _____ / __ / _____ (Today is Tuesday). The children take turns guessing letters. If correct, the teacher fills in the blank or blanks if the letter appears more than once. If incorrect, she puts a cross under the blank. The children get as many turns to guess as there are blanks in the sentence.

If, during the game, a child thinks he knows the sentence, even though it's incomplete, he may guess. If correct, the class gains two points. If not, it loses two blanks on the sentence. If they complete the sentence by guessing the letters, they gain one point.

Scrambled Eggs: Use words from the children's spelling list and scramble the letters. Ask them to unscramble the letters and write the word correctly.

Building Words: Write a long word on the board, such as "construction" or "transportation." Around holiday times, use the name of the holiday.

Each child makes as many words as he can from the letters in the word. This game can also be played in teams.

Another Word-Building Game: Choose two captains and have them choose teams. Each team has the use of the five vowels. As a class they decide on eight or ten consonants. These are listed on the board. The teams then write down as many words as they can using the vowels and the consonants on the board.

Score it or not. It's fun to play.

IF YOU USE THE TEXT AND NEED ADDITIONAL WORK— PRIMARY GRADES

Categories

List on the board several categories, for example, food, transportation, animals, colors, real, or make believe. Refer to the reading book being used and list words appropriate for these categories. Children copy the categories and then list the words in the appropriate columns.

As variations the children can look through the text to find words on their own to fit the categories or the children can draw pictures under each category instead of finding words.

Text Vocabulary

Copy a list of words from the text on the board. Leave out vowels. Ask the children to write the words on their papers, filling in the vowels.

Following Directions

Here is a sample assignment to write on the board:

> Make three airplanes
> Make four fathers
> Make five fathers

Refer to the pre-primer for appropriate vocabulary. Ask the children to follow the instructions by drawing on paper.

For older children the directions can be more complicated, for example, make two boys, make one girl, put one girl in the middle.

IF YOU USE THE TEXT AND NEED ADDITIONAL WORK— UPPER GRADES

Story Vocabulary

List new words in the story (found at the end of the basic reading book). The children look in the story for sentences containing those words. They can either write the sentence and underline the word or mark the page and paragraph number. The children add suitable suffixes to the words. The teacher lists words from the story that have prefixes or suffixes and the children underline the root word.

List contractions. The children write the two words that make up the contraction. Or do the opposite—list the two words and have the children write contractions.

List compound words. The children write the two words that

make up the compound word. Or put on the board two lists that can be used to make compound words, and have the children match the appropriate words.

Using words from the text, have the children write antonyms or synonyms.

After checking the vocabulary of a specific story, the teacher makes her own list of words on the board and the children refer to the story to find their antonyms or synonyms.

Questions about a Story

Make up questions about a story in the reader or have the children make up their own. They can exchange with neighbors to write answers. You can use the basics of who, when, where, and what happened. This saves you from reading the story if time is short. Questions can be in the form of multiple choice, true or false, or fill-in blanks.

With more mature groups, discuss the meaning of conflict and resolution in plots of stories. Have them analyze stories for those points.

Panel of Experts

Four or five children volunteer to be experts on a panel. The experts study the story carefully, while the rest of the class writes questions about the story. At the end of the preparation time, questions can be asked of the panel by a moderator or by children individually. (Panel of Experts is a very successful technique to use in social studies or science or whenever there is a body of information to be mastered.)

Summarizing

Here are a number of activities that will help children learn the skills of summarizing:

☐ Summarize a story in cartoon form.

☐ Write a summary of one paragraph. First discuss the qualities of a good summary, emphasizing the need to

include only the main points of the story.
- ☐ Outline the story.
- ☐ Write captions for pictures in the story.
- ☐ Write a different ending for the story.
- ☐ Illustrate the story.
- ☐ If the story is suitable, dramatize it.
- ☐ Make an illustrated map of the setting of the story.

MATERIALS NOT USUALLY FOUND IN CLASSROOMS

ALPHABET ACTIVITIES
Block letter patterns (optional).
One deck of alphabet cards (upper case).
One deck of alphabet cards (lower case).

CREATIVE WRITING
Old glove.
Medallion.
Art prints or magazine pictures.

BOOKS

Arbuthnot, May H. *Arbuthnot Anthology of Children's Literature,* rev. ed. Chicago: Scott,Foresman, 1971.

de Regniers, Beatrice, and others. *Poems Children Will Sit Still For.* New York: Citation Press, 1969, paperback.

Lear, Edward. *The Complete Nonsense of Edward Lear.* New York: Dover Publications, 1951, paperback.

O'Neill, Mary. *Hailstones and Halibut Bones.* New York: Doubleday, 1961.

Parish, Peggy. *Amelia Bedelia.* New York: Scholastic Book Services, 1966, paperback.

Ward, Winifred. *Stories to Dramatize.* Anchorage: Anchorage Press, 1952.

If you have a flair for drama, don't mind noise, movement, or mess, and welcome the unpredictable, this chapter is for you.

SCAVENGER HUNT

Have the children pick partners. Give each pair a list of questions to be answered. The questions can be written on the board, or you may want to have a supply of duplicated copies with you.

Here are some suggested questions:

☐ List three things in the room that are smooth.

☐ What is the color of the substitute's eyes?

☐ Draw a lovely flower.

☐ How many minutes are there between 3:30 p.m. and 4:45 a.m.?

☐ How many red stripes are there in the American flag?

☐ How many doors are there in the classroom?

☐ How many windows are there in the classroom?

☐ How many blue-eyed people are in the class?

☐ How many children wear braces?

☐ How many children in the class have last names beginning with "S"?

☐ How many children have first names beginning with "T"?

☐ How many of the last names in the class have two syllables?

If there are dictionaries in the room, add some questions that require dictionary work.

If there is a map, add some questions that require map work. For example, "What is the capital of Oregon?"

If there are encyclopedias available, add some questions that can be researched quickly.

DO A MURAL IN A DAY

Some suggestions for materials are pastels, chalk, crayon, cut paper (for a mosaic mural) and a long sheet of heavy paper. These materials can be used together. They are usually available in classrooms and are easy to organize.

Let the group discuss the theme of their mural. Some suggested subjects are:

☐ Fantasy flowers in a fantasy forest

☐ Fantasy animals

☐ Prehistoric animals

☐ Circus

☐ Zoo

☐ City of the future (including futuristic cars and planes)

☐ Anything of interest that the group is studying.

One method of working is to fill in the background directly on the heavy paper and draw the figures on separate paper. Cut out the figures and glue them to the background. This method allows everyone to work at the same time.

Another method is to do the background directly, sketch the figures on it, and then complete the figures.

If you use the mosaic method, put in the background first. (Regardless of which method you use, put in the background first as it's too difficult to work around the figures afterward.) The materials for a mosaic can be prepared by children cutting or tearing the paper. Children need to be made aware of creating contrasting areas (large pieces against small ones or dark against light).

A third method of working is to divide the mural paper into segments that are asymmetrical. Each child or pair has a segment to work on. Each child's section is complete in itself but is based on the overall theme.

If the art materials are not easily accessible, then a chalk mural can be done on the chalkboard. Stress contrasting textures, which can be made with the chalk by making dots, lines, crosses, and working the chalk on its side.

PUBLISH A NEWSPAPER IN A DAY

Tell the children you would like to try publishing a newspaper in one day.

Decide on the kinds of topics to go in the paper, such as:
- ☐ TV and movie reviews
- ☐ Pet stories
- ☐ Accident reports
- ☐ Sports commentary
- ☐ Feature stories
- ☐ Interviews (pretend)
- ☐ Dear Abby letters
- ☐ News of the school
- ☐ Advertisements
- ☐ Cartoons

The children will think of others.

Ask for volunteers to be editors for the various topics or departments. It relieves the burden for some children to be co-editors.

Each child selects a subject to write about. You will have to see that the topics are well distributed. When the articles are written, and headlines added, the children give their pieces to the appropriate editor who corrects as much as he can. The teacher acts as chief editor and makes final corrections.

While children are busy writing their articles, arrange the printing room. If available, use large paper that is lined. If there isn't any, use this time to quickly line blank paper using a yardstick or chart liner. If neither of these materials is available, use the blackboard. The paper can be tacked to bulletin boards, taped to blackboards, or placed on the floor.

After articles are approved and corrected, the editor assigns the writers to print their pieces on lined paper. The paper should be arranged in columns as in a newspaper. It's advisable to pencil in the text first and then go over it with a pen.

This activity can take a full day, and you will be covering reading, creative writing, language skills, handwriting—everything.

INSTANT THEATER

Read the children a short story in which the action and characters are clearly defined, i.e., fairy tales or folk tales. A good source is *Stories to Dramatize* by Winifred Ward.

List the characters on the board with the children. Establish a sequence of scenes with them and where the action will take place in the room.

Ask for volunteers to play the various roles and immediately begin the action. There need be no rehearsal; the dialogue is spontaneous. After the presentation, evaluate it *briefly* with the children, stressing who stayed in character, i.e., with facial expressions, body movement, voice quality, and dialogue.

Choose a second cast to act out the story again. When the play goes well the first time, it fires the enthusiasm of the other children, so choose outgoing children to play the important parts in the first try.

You can also divide the class into groups. Have each group work on the same story, but present its own interpretation. All the children can participate in the planning at the same time, and later they enjoy watching each other. You'll be surprised at the varied interpretations.

PAPER BAG PUPPET SHOW

Divide the class into five groups. Each group decides on a story. They can make up their own or you can read them a story and ask each group to interpret it. Each group decides the characters they need. The characters are created from a paper bag. (Paper lunch sacks are available in markets and often in the school.)

The face is drawn on the bottom of the bag with the mouth on the fold of the flap. A child puts his hand in the bag with his fingers in the fold. When he opens and closes the flap, the puppet appears to be talking. If paste and colored paper are available, glue on eyelashes, ears, or noses.

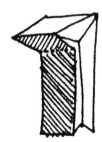

When the puppets are ready, give the children time to rehearse, using a table for a stage. A chart rack also makes a good stage because the children can hide behind it.

VOCABULARY DEVELOPMENT—PRIMARY GRADES

Bring along a list of words you wish to introduce, for example, "countenance," "clammer," "pachoderm," "chanticleer," "haunches," "enraged," "ecstatic," "awkward," or "cautious."

Capture the children's attention by saying, "I know only big words." Say a word like "countenance." Dramatize the word in some way. Tell the children you're going to put your hand on your countenance, do so. Tell them you're going to make a happy countenance, do so. Do the same with a sad countenance, and so on. See if the children can figure out the meaning of the word.

Here are some other suggestions for demonstrating words:
- [ ] Clammer—make a lot of noise beating on something or yelling.
- [ ] Pachoderm—walk heavily, pretending to have a trunk.
- [ ] Chanticleer—crow.
- [ ] Haunches—sit on your haunches or have a child squat and tell the class he is sitting on his haunches.
- [ ] Enraged—stamp your feet, make an angry face, yell, shake your fist.
- [ ] Ecstatic—jump with joy, talk about how happy you are, let your face and body show it.
- [ ] Awkward—bump into things, trip, dance clumsily.
- [ ] Cautious—pretend to be crossing the street very carefully.

Let the children take turns dramatizing the words in their own way. At the end of the day, you might take a few minutes to see if they recall the words and their meanings.

To make this work, you have to drop your inhibitions and let yourself go.

RADIO PLAYS

Discuss the difference between radio plays and TV plays. Emphasize the importance of sound effects and vocal expression in the former. Talk about how to make sound effects in a classroom situation. What things are available for making sounds? Use your own body and voice to stamp, clap, and imitate sounds and use things in the room like slamming doors, crunching paper, and tapping rulers. The children will come up with their own ideas.

Divide the class into five groups. Each group selects a story. They can make up their own, or you can read them a story and have each group interpret it. Each group should decide on the characters, sequence, and sound effects needed. When all the groups are ready, tape one presentation at a time while the others watch and listen.

FASHION SHOW

In this activity the children draw and cut out a figure large enough to hide behind with only their faces showing. You will need to bring in a large roll of heavy paper. Each child cuts out a piece large enough to cover his entire body. At the top he cuts out an oval where his face can fit snugly. Around the cut-out face, he creates a hair-do or headdress.

On the lower part of the paper the children design new clothes. They can use any materials available to decorate their creations such as buttons, belts, or flowers made from additional paper.

To "wear" the costume, the child can cut holes and place his arms through them or he can simply hold the paper in front of him as it will be suspended from his face.

This activity can be used as an opener. It makes for instant rapport. Do the art work, then change the tempo to something more structured, and have a fashion show later on in the day. If possible, use a musical background as children display their fashions one by one.

If there isn't enough room to do life-size fashions, then do a head and torso or just a hairdo.

DESIGNING PAPER AIRPLANES

Stage a paper airplane flying contest with two events: distance contest and sailing through a target.

Materials are readily available in every classroom: paper, scissors, staplers, maybe glue, tape, pins, and paper clips.

Discuss with the children ideas for workable designs. Some suggestions are: the shape of the plane should be long and narrow, coming to a point; paper clips can be used to hold the parts together; the front end can be weighted with a pin, which helps the glider to sail.

Let children name their planes.

Distance Event: Each contestant sails his plane from a starting point. Mark each landing with the name of the plane.

Target Event: Use a clothes hanger bent into the shape of a circle. Leave the hook at the top. Hang it up, if possible. If not, a child can hold it. Contestants try to sail their gliders through the target from a starting point. For final eliminations, move the starting point further back.

This also makes a good opener. Construct the planes, shift to a more structured activity, and hold the contests later on in the day. With this prospect in view, you'll really give the children something to look forward to.

SENSE AWARENESS

Bring two or three unlabelled bottles containing strong smelling substances such as vinegar, vanilla, garlic, or Clorox. Place bottles on the desk in front of the room. Have the children come up with pencil and paper, smell each bottle, and write down what they think it is without discussing it.

After the class has identified the odors, discuss with them how we are dependent on our sense of smell. Discuss the relationship between taste and smell. The following experiment will help clarify it. Using two foods with similar textures, like apples and pears, have a few children, with eyes closed, hold their noses and try to identify which fruit they are eating. Have them open their eyes to verify.

This experiment can lead into a discussion of how other senses such as hearing and seeing, orient us. Talk about how people who have lost their hearing manage by lip reading and sign language. If possible bring in copies of the deaf alphabet; local schools for the deaf are good sources. The children can practice the deaf alphabet and try to communicate with each other using it. When they feel competent, they can create a message, which the class tries to interpret.

To develop an awareness of the difficulties of blindness, ask the children to memorize the room in terms of a clock. Decide on a point in the room that is 12 o'clock. Then the children choose partners. One is blindfolded (have enough blindfolds for half the class), and the other watches to make sure his "blind" friend does not hurt himself. Ask the blindfolded children to walk to a certain object or area in the room. It will be interesting to see how they manage. Afterwards, ask them to describe their feelings. Then partners can change roles.

For a similar experience, the blindfolded children can be led someplace outside the room such as the play yard. This involves trusting one's partner. An interesting discussion will certainly follow.

SIGNALING

Have the children choose partners. Put the Morse Code on the board or bring out a chart or prepared dittos. Unless you have dittos, the children must make their own copies from the board or chart.

Partners decide on a way to distinguish between dots and dashes, i. e., a snap of the finger for a dot and a clap of the hands for a dash. Let partners practice identifying each other's letters. When they are ready to practice words, they should write them down. If they seem to be catching on, let them try simple sentences.

International Morse Code

A •–	J •–––	S •••	1 •––––
B –•••	K –•–	T –	2 ••–––
C –•–•	L •–••	U ••–	3 •••––
D –••	M ––	V •••–	4 ••••–
E •	N –•	W •––	5 •••••
F ••–•	O –––	X –••–	6 –••••
G ––•	P •––•	Y –•––	7 ––•••
H ••••	Q ––•–	Z ––••	8 –––••
I ••	R •–•		9 ––––•
			0 –––––

MATERIALS NOT USUALLY FOUND IN CLASSROOMS

SCAVENGER HUNT
Duplicated copies of questions.

PAPER BAG PUPPET SHOW
Enough paper bags for the class.

RADIO PLAYS
Tape recorder.

DESIGNING PAPER AIRPLANES
Wire clothes hanger.

SENSE AWARENESS
Two or three bottles with vinegar, Clorox, vanilla, or other strong smelling substances.
Apple and pear.
Deaf alphabet.
Cloths for blindfolds.

SIGNALING
Morse Code ditto (optional).

BOOKS

Ward, Winifred. *Stories to Dramatize*. Anchorage: Anchorage Press, 1952.

GEOGRAPHY

Detectives

MATERIALS: Paper and pencils.

A criminal has escaped from jail. The children are detectives trying to track him down. Clues are given in geographic hints. For example:

1. The crime was committed in the southernmost port city of California.
2. The fugitive was seen by the police in the desert gambling city in southern Nevada.
3. He hid out in the Grand Canyon State.
4. He struggled across the longest mountain range in the United States and stayed overnight in the state whose capital is Cheyenne.
5. He traveled down the longest river in the United States.
6. At the mouth of this river he took a boat to the Peninsula State.

7. Driving on the East Coast his car broke down in the nation's capital.
8. He made his way to the automobile manufacturing city on Lake Erie to buy a new car.
9. He crossed the largest of the Great Lakes.
10. The fugitive was apprehended trying to cross the river bordering the United States and Mexico.

After working out these sample clues, have the children make up their own escape routes (using the geography text and maps), exchange papers, and solve each other's problems.

The above clues obviously involve United States geography, but any area the children are studying can be used to make up clues.

If blank maps are available, the children can mark the fugitive's escape route.

Panel of Experts

MATERIALS: Geography text, paper, pencils.

Four or five children volunteer to be experts on a panel. Select a chapter from the social studies text. Everybody reads the chapter. The experts study the chapter, or small sections of it carefully, while the rest of the class writes up questions about the chapter (or section). At the end of the preparation time, questions can be asked of the panel by a moderator who reads the children's questions, or individuals can ask their own questions.

If anyone in the class disagrees with an expert's answer, his challenge must be supported by references from the text.

Where Am I?

MATERIALS: Social studies texts.

Briefly review latitude and longitude. Then, using a map from a social studies text, call out a reference. Alone, or with partners, the children check their maps and write down the location indicated by the latitude and longitude.

The children can take turns giving the class reference points on the map.

Mapping the Classroom

MATERIALS: Compass, pencil, papers.

Ask the children which way is north. There will be much disagreement. Verify the proper direction with a compass. The children can then establish the directions in the room using the compass.

Point out that maps show north at the top, therefore the northern part of the room should go at the top of their paper. Ask the children to notice what is in the northern part of their room, i.e., the blackboard or windows. Point out that this is what should appear at the top of their classroom maps. Do the same with the other directions.

Discuss the use of symbols on a map and the function of a key. Use an available large map or sketch a simple map of the room on the board to demonstrate how the key gives meaning to the symbols.

As a group, decide on the important things to include when making a map of the room. Have them decide individually or as a group (depending on maturity) on the symbols they will use for closets, windows, doors, blackboards, and other features of the room. After this discussion, each child makes a map of the room.

Older children can make a map of the entire school. Take a walk around the school. Decide on the directions. List the important elements of the school to include. Decide on symbols.

You can also ask the children to draw a map of a room in their house or apartment that they know well, showing directions and using symbols and a key.

Mapping an Imaginary Land

MATERIALS: Large paper, pencils, crayons.

Elicit from the children geographic features they know and

list them on the board, for example, mountains, lakes, rivers, coastline, islands, deserts, cities, highways, or railroads.

Give out large pieces of paper and ask the children to draw a picture of an imaginary land which includes the geographical features listed. Then ask them to draw a map of their picture on a much smaller piece of paper. They will have to scale down items from the large picture and use colors and symbols to represent others. They should include a key to translate their symbols and colors.

Map Symbols

MATERIALS: Pencils, paper.

On the blackboard write the symbols listed below. Briefly go over them with the children and ask them to categorize them according to man-made and natural features.

Ask them to draw an island and place these features on it as they might appear on an actual island.

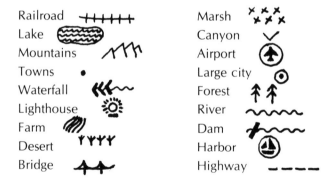

Railroad Marsh
Lake Canyon
Mountains Airport
Towns Large city
Waterfall Forest
Lighthouse River
Farm Dam
Desert Harbor
Bridge Highway

Creating a Travel Brochure

MATERIALS: Drawing paper, coloring materials, sample travel brochures.

Discuss with the class the format of a typical travel brochure. Show them ones you have brought in and then talk about other possible arrangements such as a fold out, book form, or leaflet. Point out the use of attractive colors, slogans, pictures of scenery, listings of sites and historical places, pertinent facts about the area, and inclusion of a map.

Use an area the children know about from their social studies work. List the kinds of information they already know that can be used in a brochure and determine what needs more research.

After the research period, list the additional information on the board. With all this data, the children can create their own travel brochures.

HISTORY

Writing a Social Studies Book

MATERIALS: Pencils, paper, coloring materials.

This project is geared for fifth- and sixth-graders since it makes use of concepts from their level of social studies.

The children can write and illustrate their own books based on an outline you give them. If they like, they can work as co-authors.

Write the italic parts of the following outline on the board. Explain the other portions orally.

Create a Mythical Country

Chapter I — *Decide on a name for your country.* It should not be a fantasy or fairy land. The name should have some historical significance. *Describe and illustrate the geographical features* such as topography, island or mainland, climate, natural resources, bodies of water, main cities, and so on. *Draw a map of this country* showing as much of the above information as possible. *Design a flag, currency, stamps, and a national motto.*

Chapter II — *Your country's vital overland trade routes have been suddenly closed. Why?* The reason must be realistic, such as war in the area or a natural catastrophe. Since your country cannot win this war, it must send out explorers to search for a new trade route.

Chapter III — *Name the explorer. Draw his portrait. Describe his route. Draw a map to show it. Describe his trip. Tell what he found. Name the new land.* Give the reason for the name.

Chapter IV — *Describe and illustrate the geography of the new land. What are the people like? Make a map of the land.*

This is a good stopping place, but the project can be developed further.

Chapter V — *Colonies are established. Map them. Describe and show what the colonists look like.* Tell why they came and what their life is like in the new land.

Chapter VI — *Describe and illustrate the life of the native inhabitants.* Tell how the colonists got along with the native population and the problems they faced.

Chapter VII — *Conflict develops with the mother country.* Describe the colonists' struggle for independence.

To organize the completed book, make a cover, give the chapters titles, and arrange a table of contents.

Biography

MATERIALS: Pencils and paper.

This is a matching game using the personalities of history. Have the children use their texts, if necessary, to suggest a list of important personalities. Write the names on the board.

The number of people should equal half the number of children in the class.

The children research an important fact or event connected with each name. They write the information on one side of a paper—it should be short. The name of the personality is written at the very bottom of the page. While the children are working, write each historical name on a separate piece of paper. When they are finished, scan the papers and use the best one for each name. Tear off the name written on the bottom of the page. Discard it, but use the ones you have written.

Distribute the names and information at random, face down on the children's desks. At a signal, they turn them over and try to match names and information. When they do, they sit down together. After everyone has found his match, each pair can name the personality and give the matching information.

Dramatizing Historical Events

MATERIALS: None.

Discuss episodes in history that are colorful and lend themselves to dramatization. For example, the voyages of Columbus, Ponce de Leon and the Fountain of Youth, the "Mayflower" and Pilgrims, John Smith and Pocahontas, the Boston Tea Party, Harriet Tubman and the Underground Railroad, or many others.

Divide the class into about five committees. They each decide on an episode to dramatize. Any necessary research can be done from the social studies book.

After a practice period, the groups settle down to watch each other's skits.

In the primary grades the children can dramatize the jobs of community helpers, firemen, policemen, librarians and so forth.

INTERNATIONAL PROJECTS

Flags

MATERIALS: Ten–fifteen pictures or drawings of flags from around the world, mural paper, drawing paper, coloring materials, toothpicks.

The larger the flag pictures the better. (Children will love to make the flags for you during a subbing day before you use this activity.)

Help the children identify the flags of the various countries. Select a group of six to eight children to do a freehand map of the world on the mural paper. The remaining children can make the minature flags. These must be quite small so that they can be attached to toothpicks.

While the flag-makers are at work, you may need to help the map-makers.

When both groups are finished, the children get together and decide where to place the flags.

As a variation, make United States state flags and make a freehand drawing of the United States. Another idea is to ask each child to make a poster using as many flags as he wishes.

Stamps

MATERIALS: About thirty-five stamps from foreign countries, paper, coloring materials, pencils.

Distribute one stamp, attached to a sheet of paper, to each child. Ask the children to make a list of the kinds of information they can find out about the country from their stamps. For example, words on the stamp can give a clue to the language of the country and illustrations can show products, clothing, events in history, climate, famous people, and so forth.

Ask some of the children to report on their findings. They should tell which clues on their stamps are the basis for their statements.

After sharing the information with the class, ask the children to design a stamp of their own, which will reflect the history or geography of the country they are studying. These should be made on large sheets of paper, using color.

International Games

List, with the children, familiar games which need no equipment. If the children do not include simple Simon or hot and cold, add them to the list.

After the list is finished, tell the children that you will show them how the children in Germany play a version of simple Simon. Introduce commandant (see instructions below). Allow the children to play. Then show them how to play the other foreign games (see instructions below). After each one, ask the children if they see any similarities to games on their list.

The children might want to make up some games of their own. Talk briefly with them about what makes a good game—challenge, organization, and rules. Break up into four or five committees. After the planning period is over, have each committee present its game and have everyone play it.

Commandant (Commander) — Germany

MATERIALS: None.

This game is like simple Simon. The leader (Commander) uses only four movements:

Timber—alternate tapping with index fingers on edge of desk
Hammer—fist pounding on desk
Ax—side of hand hitting desk
Saw—flat palm moving back and forth on desk

The leader says "Commander" and names one of the movements. The leader also does the movement. The children must follow the verbal instruction *only* when it is preceded by the word "Commander." The leader tries to confuse the children by omitting the word "Commander" or by saying one movement and doing another.

As children make mistakes, they are eliminated. The game continues until one person is left.

Jan, Ken, Po—Japan

MATERIALS: None.

Divide the group into two teams, each with a captain. The captains decide on a symbol—stone, paper or scissor:

Stone—closed fist

Paper—open hand

Scissors—two extended fingers

Each team lines up with their hands behind their backs. The captain passes the symbol down to the next person on his team, making sure that it is hidden from the other team. Each team member passes what he receives to the next person. When all have received the symbol, both teams face each other with their right fist closed. All together they chant, "Jan, Ken, Po." At the word "Po," they extend their right hands, showing the symbol they have received. The most powerful symbol wins:

Stone wins over scissors, because stone dulls scissors.

Scissors wins over paper, because scissors cuts paper.

Paper wins over stone, because paper wraps stone.

If both teams use the same symbol, neither wins. A point is scored for each win. The game continues until each member of the team has had a turn being captain and choosing the symbol.

As a variation, pairs of children can play by themselves.

Straight Face—Native American

MATERIALS: None.

Boys and girls separate into two teams. Each team chooses a leader. The boys' leader is called Brave, the girls' leader, Squaw. The Brave assigns numbers to the boys, the Squaw does the same with the girls. Each teams' numbers are kept secret.

The teams line up at opposite ends of the room facing each other. The Brave and Squaw each call a number. The team members having those numbers must walk toward each other. Just as they pass each other the boy must say, "My dear Squaw," and the girl must say, "My dear Brave." The object is to keep a straight face. If either one laughs or smiles, his team gets a mark. The team with the fewest marks wins. The game continues until all numbers have been called.

Hot and Cold—African Style

MATERIALS: Small objects found in the room and pencils.

One person is IT and goes out of the room. An object is hidden. IT returns and tries to find the object.

To show IT how close he is to the object, the other children drum on their desks with pencils. The closer IT is to the object, the louder the drumming.

This can be played with a leader conducting the drumming.

Stadt, Land, Fluss (City, Country, River)—Germany

MATERIALS: Paper and pencils.

The children divide their papers into categories such as city, country, river, mountains, states, or other geographical entities.

Choose one person to recite the alphabet to himself. At a signal, the child stops and tells the class which letter he has reached.

The children, using books or not (depending on their ability), write down appropriate entries for the categories on their papers. Entries must begin with the letter called. After a reasonable time, stop and score.

One point is given for each correct entry, and five points for an entry nobody else has.

Other categories such as famous names, foods, occupations, cars, and so on can be substituted for geographical terms. Younger children can handle these categories.

RESEARCH SKILLS

Choosing Key Words

MATERIALS: Paper, pencils, social studies or science book.

Choose a paragraph from an available social studies or science book, and write it on the board. Do this when the children are occupied with something else or are out of the room.

Discuss the skill of note taking, which involves identifying key words or phrases. Using the paragraph on the board, ask the children to suggest words or phrases that could be eliminated without destroying the sense of the paragraph. Erase those words. Ask the children to reconstruct the paragraph orally.

Note Taking

MATERIALS: Paper, pencils, social studies or science books.

Assign a paragraph from an available book. Distribute one-inch wide strips of paper. Using this strip of paper, the children try to take notes on the paragraph. Challenge them to take notes on only one side of the strip.

When they are finished, ask them to use these notes to reconstruct the paragraph in their own words.

Share the paragraphs orally. The variations will be interesting.

Writing Headlines

MATERIALS: Paper, pencils, short newspaper or magazine article or social studies text.

Talk with the children about the function of a headline — to capture attention by expressing the main idea in a few descriptive words.

Read an interesting short article to the class. It can be from a current magazine or newspaper or a social studies book. Ask the children to write headlines for the article. Have them read their work aloud to each other.

TIME LINE

MATERIALS: A large packet of pictures of historical episodes, famous people, machines, or other kinds of things that can be placed in a time sequence.

The pictures should be stapled on cards and placed in a box.

Draw a line down the center of a long piece of paper. Divide it into centuries or half centuries. Place it on the floor and have the children sit on either side of the paper.

Each child takes a turn picking out a card. The idea is to try to place the card in its appropriate time period.

This activity will generate heated discussions. Available books or you will be the resource for verification.

CURRENT EVENTS

Who Am I?

MATERIALS: A collection of photographs of people in the news — political figures, TV personalities, sports and movie stars, and the like, paper, pencils.

This can be scored by giving a point for each correct category answer. However, it need not be scored. After all the pictures have been shown, you can show them again, asking for oral responses from the class.

Ask the children to work as partners. Give out paper, which the children fold in half. They title one column, "Who Am I?" and the other, "What Have I Done?"

Hold up a picture. The partners decide what they know about the person and write his name and achievements down under the appropriate headings.

Headlines in the News

MATERIALS: Headlines cut from current newspaper or magazines, paper, pencils.

Hold up a headline and read it to the group. Have the children prepare a short article that they think fits the headline, using as much information as they have. If they feel they don't have any actual information about the events, they can write about what the headline suggests. This should produce some interesting material.

Share aloud the articles the children have written. Then read the actual article that goes with the headline.

As a variation, read short articles and have the children write headlines.

Pictures in the News

MATERIALS: Collection of action pictures from newspapers and magazines (some with captions and some without), pencils, paper.

Show some of the pictures and read their captions, pointing out how they tell what is happening in few words. Next, show pictures without captions and have the children try to write their own.

Match the Headline

MATERIALS: Articles and headlines from a Sunday newspaper.

Select about twenty articles of varying subject matter. Cut apart the headline from the article, and staple each part to a separate piece of paper. (For your own quick checking purposes, list the headline and the first few words of the article on a separate sheet).

Distribute headlines and articles at random to the class.

At a signal, the children circulate trying to match their headlines with the articles and vice versa. As soon as two children think they're matched, they come up to you to be checked. Then they sit down. When all have been matched, collect the articles and headlines, shuffle, and have the class play again.

PRIMARY ACTIVITIES

Safe Driving

MATERIALS: Chalk.

Discuss with the children the rules of safe driving and the need to obey them. Make sure they talk about signaling, passing on the left, exiting on the right, speed limits, tailgating, knowing how to enter the flow of traffic, and the role of the policeman in enforcing these rules.

Next the children choose to be a passenger car or truck. Those wanting to be trucks should work in pairs, one as the cab and the other as the trailer. Choose two cruising policemen.

Take the children to the play yard. Mark a circle or rectangle to represent a lane of the freeway. The children line up around the area. They go around it trying to follow the freeway rules. If they wish to pass, they must signal and pass on the left. If they wish to exit, they must do it on the right, and so on. The exits should be marked on the circle or rectangle.

The policemen cruise and control traffic, giving tickets when necessary. They cruise inside the main circle. Policemen must explain the offense before giving a ticket. Children receiving tickets can be kept off the freeway for a short time.

Making Butter

MATERIALS: Quart jar with tight lid, one-half pint of whipping cream, knife, and crackers.

Discuss dairy products and their source. If this is a new experience for the children, have them discuss how they think butter is made.

Follow the directions given in Chapter 1, page 14.

Go Fish

MATERIALS: Pictures of related categories such as wild animals—

domesticated animals, the four seasons, real and make-believe, fruits and vegetables, long ago—the present—the future, and the like, ruler, paper clips, magnet, cards for mounting pictures, string, box.

Cut out the pictures and mount them on cards. On each card fasten a paper clip. Make a fishing pole out of a ruler with a string attached. Tie a magnet to the end of the string. Put the cards in a box.

Write each category of pictures on a piece of paper and arrange them on the floor. If possible, have the children sit in a circle around the fishing box. Each child takes a turn fishing a picture out of the box. He tries to place it on the proper category card on the floor.

Making an Information Table

MATERIALS: Drawing paper and coloring materials.

Talk with the children about the kinds of jobs held by adults they know and who benefits from what these people do.

Give the children large pieces of drawing paper and have them divide them into thirds. Ask them to label the first column *People,* the second *Jobs,* and the third *Who is Helped.*

The children use pictures to illustrate each category. When all are finished, have a sharing time.

Murals

MATERIALS: Mural paper, drawing paper, coloring materials, paste.

Making murals can enrich the current social studies unit being studied. With the children pick out the visual highlights of a chapter or unit, for instance:

- ☐ Harbors—kinds of boats, shape of harbor, lighthouses, islands
- ☐ Transportation—trains, trucks, cars, airplanes
- ☐ Community Workers—bakers, waitresses, carpenters, electricians, plumbers, policemen, and so on

☐ Community Helpers—postmen, firemen, policemen, librarians, and so forth

☐ Barnyard Animals—ducks, cows, sheep, horses, chickens, and the like

☐ Wild Animals—lions, deer, squirrels, and so on

Talk with the children about what activities could be going on in any category. List these on the board. Have volunteers make individual drawings that will be cut out and pasted on the mural. While the individual drawings are being made, select a group to color in the background for the mural.

MATERIALS NOT USUALLY FOUND IN CLASSROOMS

MAPPING THE CLASSROOM

Compass.

CREATING A TRAVEL BROCHURE

Samples of travel brochures.

FLAGS

Kit of ten or fifteen pictures of flags of the world, The United Nations Flag Kit ($2.98) and Flags of the U.N. ($.75), may be purchased from the United Nations, Sales Section, Publishing Service, New York, N.Y. 10017.

Pictures are also found in most encyclopedias.

Toothpicks.

STAMPS

About thirty-five foreign stamps. Inexpensive packets may be bought from most stamp dealers.

TIME LINE

Packet of pictures of historical episodes, famous people, well-known inventions, or any information that can be placed in a time sequence.

WRITING HEADLINES

A few short current articles.

WHO AM I?

Collection of photographs of people in the news—political figures, sports, movie and TV people.

HEADLINES IN THE NEWS

Current articles and headlines.

PICTURES IN THE NEWS

Collection of action pictures from magazines and newspapers—some with captions.

MATCH THE HEADLINE

About twenty articles and accompanying headlines.

MAKING BUTTER

Quart jar with tight lid.
One-half pint whipping cream.
Knife.
Crackers.

GO FISH

Pictures of related categories:
   Wild and domesticated animals
   Four seasons
   Real and make-believe
   Fruits and vegetables
   Long ago, present, future
Magnet.
String.
Box.

MATHEMATICS

The numerology activities described in the Openers Chapter would also be appropriate for math classes (see pages 7–9).

STRATEGY

MATERIALS: Blackboard.

This game is like tic tac toe. The object is to get four points in a straight line.

Draw a grid on the blackboard of this shape or larger.

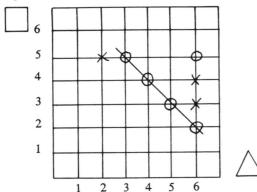

The numbers on the vertical will be called box numbers and those on the horizontal triangle numbers. A box number is called first, then a triangle number. For practice, have individual children call out an ordered pair and place the points on the grid. This is to give them the experience of placing points accurately on a grid.

Erase the practice grid and draw a new one. At first the teacher can play against the class.

One child calls a point. The teacher marks it on the grid with an X. Next, the teacher calls a point and chooses a child to mark it with a small circle. Both children and teacher try to block each other and at the same time try to get four points in a line.

Groups or pairs of children can then draw their own grids and play the game themselves.

TREASURE HUNT

MATERIALS: Two pieces of graph paper for each child, if available. Otherwise the children make their own graph papers by simply crossing horizontal and vertical lines.

This game is played in pairs. The object is to dig up the other person's treasure.

On each of the two graphs have the children label the vertical lines with numbers and the horizontal lines with letters. Name one graph "My Treasure" and the other "Opponent's Treasure"

On the "My Treasure" graph, each player buries a treasure chest by placing four Xs on four points forming a straight line. On other points forming straight lines a pot of gold is buried with three Xs and a bag of jewels with two Xs. Leave the other graph blank. It is to record guesses.

The first player calls three points, such as B–6, F–3, and J–2 to see if he can uncover his opponent's treasure. As he calls these points, he records them on his graph labeled "Op-

Opponent's Treasure
(record your calls)

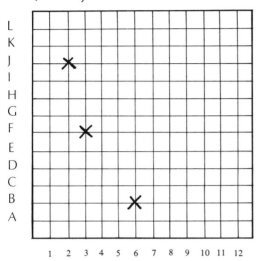

My Treasure

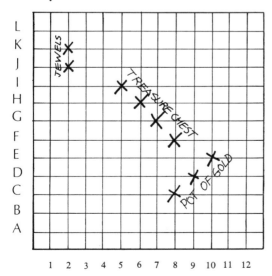

ponent's Treasure." After his three calls, his opponent must tell if any of his treasures have been discovered and which ones they are. He does <u>not</u> tell which calls made the discoveries. The caller should note carefully the points he has called. He will use them in planning future calls.

Now the other player becomes the caller. The two players alternate in calling until one of them has dug up all the other's treasure.

DOT DESIGNS

MATERIALS: Graph paper, pencils.

Have the children label the vertical lines on the graph with numbers and the horizontal lines with letters.

Tell them you are going to call out points on the graph and that they are to place a dot on those points. The first point should be labeled 1, the second point 2, and so on. You might use the following simple design or make up your own. After all the points have been called, have the children correct the numbered dots in sequence.

The children can then plot their own design and call the points to a partner or to the class.

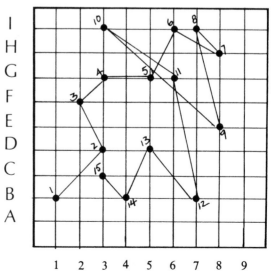

MAKING A BAR GRAPH

MATERIALS: Paper and pencil

   Write the months of the year on the board. Have the children come up two or three at a time and write their names under their birthday months.

   Now draw a grid on the blackboard. Label it with the months of the year and number of children in the class. Ask how many children have a birthday in January. The information will be right there on the board. For example, if five children have a birthday in January, fill in the space for January up through five. Continue in this way with all the months of the year.

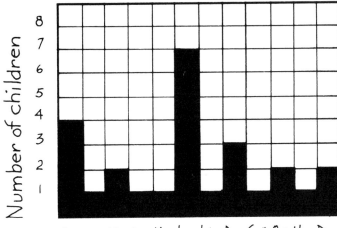

   Then have the children read the graph. Ask them how many statements they can make from the information on it. For example, which month has the most or fewest birthdays? Which season has the most? How many more children have birthdays in one month than another, and so forth.

   For the upper grades this can be a review of bar graphing. For primary children it can be a first exposure.

With upper grades, discuss what kinds of easily available information they could graph. For example, kinds of pets (this is good for primary grades, too), prevalence of letters beginning first names and last names, and the like. Have the children gather the data as a group. Put it on the board. Then the children can make their own individual graphs.

RACE AGAINST TIME

MATERIALS: A set of large flash cards, approximately 5×8 inches, with addition, subtraction, multiplication, and division combinations.

The challenge here is to see how quickly the entire class can go through the flash cards.

Select a timekeeper who will give the signal to start and call the time when the last child finishes. The teacher flashes the cards.

When a child seems to be stuck or makes a mistake, wait a few seconds and go on to the next card so that attention is not focused noticeably on the weaker children.

The class will be anxious to repeat the game to see if they can cut down their time.

As a variation ask for volunteer teams. Don't make the teams too large. If there are many children who wish to race the clock, divide them into equal teams and have them race against each other separately. Each team goes through the cards, then the next team goes, and the times are compared.

The teams can choose names—Speedy Six, Division Devils, Fearless Three, or Multiplication Masters.

For primary grades use only addition and subtraction with simple combinations.

MATCH THE NUMBER NAMES

MATERIALS: Approximately sixty 3×5 index cards or heavy paper that can be used in place of cards. Be sure there is a pair for each child in the class.

The object of this game is to match different names for the same number. The children make the game first and then play it. This is adaptable to any grade level.

Decide with the children which kinds of computations should be used in the game. For example, multiplication, division, addition, subtraction (with whole numbers or with fractions), decimal fractions and equivalents, common fractions and equivalents, and so on.

If the class decides on multiplication, have the children suggest thirty combinations and their products. List these on the board. Distribute two cards to each child. Assign each child a combination and its product. He writes the combination on one card and the answer on another. Collect all the cards. Shuffle them well.

Have the children form a big circle on the floor. Place all the cards face down on the floor. The teacher turns over the first card. Then player number one turns over a card. If the two cards should match and he recognizes that they do, he collects both and keeps them. If they don't match or if he doesn't realize that they do, the next player turns over a card. A player who, when it is his turn, recognizes a pair that has been missed may pick it up. He also then takes his own turn turning over a card. The game continues until all cards have been matched and picked up. The player with the most pairs wins.

ARITHMETIC OLYMPICS

MATERIALS: Arithmetic text or review sheets.

The object of the game is to review computations as quickly as possible.

Select one or two sections or any specific problems on a page from the text. Choose computations the children can handle pretty well. This is for review. List on the board a sequence of work to be done, for example, page 18 exercises 2 and 3 or page 25 problems 19-26.

At a signal, the children begin to work on one exercise or line of problems at a time. As they complete it, they walk up to the teacher to have their work checked. Have the answer book ready or solve the problems while the children are working.

Place a mark next to any incorrect answer. The child then has to return to his seat to correct it. If all work in an exercise is done correctly, the child goes on to the next one and follows the same procedure.

The first finished with the entire assignment takes first place and so on to as many places as you wish to have. If a child completes the work very quickly, he can help with the checking.

BETTING GAME

MATERIALS: Paper and pencils.

One side of the paper is used as a ledger, the other side as a worksheet.

Tell the children that they will each be given $5.00 with which to bet—an imaginary $5.00, of course. With this money they may place a bet, from 1¢ to $5.00 that they will correctly solve the problem put on the board.

Tell the class the kind of problem it will be. Decide how much information you want to give. For example, if it's addition, you may tell that the problem will be addition of two-digit or three-digit numerals, if multiplication, two digits by two digits, or you may want to put the problem on the board beforehand.

The children decide how much they want to bet, based on their own judgment and confidence in their skill in that operation.

On the ledger side of the paper the children write down
$5.00. Underneath, they note how much they're betting.
For example: $5.00
　　　　　　2.00

The children put their heads on their desks until the problem is written on the board. (If you want to give the children a
chance to see the problem first, eliminate this step.) At a
signal, they raise their heads and copy and solve the problem
on the work side of the paper.

After a reasonable time the pencils are put down, the problem is solved at the board, and bettors either add or subtract
their bet, depending on whether or not they solved the problem correctly.

Win	Lose
$5.00	$5.00
+ 2.00	− 2.00
$7.00	$3.00

The children place their next bet from the new amount. You
will find that some children bet rashly and find themselves
without money very soon. A loan system can be worked out.
In that way everyone stays in the game.

NUMBER NAMES

MATERIALS: Blackboard.

The object of this game is to have the children figure out
other names for a specified number.

Choose a number. Write it large in the middle of the blackboard. Have five volunteers come up to the board and list as
many combinations as they can that represent the number
listed. For example, if you write down 50, responses could
be $55 - 5$, 10×5, $100 \div 2$, $52 + (-2)$, and so on. The possibilities, of course, are endless.

At the end of a short time limit, go over the lists with the
class. Count up the different correct combinations made by

all five children. That is the score for the number 50. Mark it down on a corner of the board.

Choose another number and do the same with five other volunteers.

Depending on the level of the children, you might use fractional numbers. For example, for 1/2 they might respond with 4/8, 10/20, .5, and so on.

COUNT UP

MATERIALS: Pencils and paper.

Use the spelling list for the week or the names of the children in the class. Assign each letter of the alphabet a numerical value. You can count by 2s, or 3s. For example, A = 2, B = 4, C = 6 or the letters may be valued from 1 – 26 in alphabetical order.

Begin by calling a child's name or a word from the spelling list. The children compute the numerical value of the word. A child can then take over and call a name or a word.

FORTUNE CODES

MATERIALS: Paper and pencil.

The object is to write and decode fortunes by substituting computations for letters of the alphabet.

Have each child write a fortune on a piece of paper. Go over this simple code with the group, A = 1, B = 2, C = 3, and so on. Then have them code their fortunes. Dots separate letters and diagonals separate words. For example:
25.15.21 / 23.9.12.12 / 2.5.3.15.13.5 / 1 / 6.1.13.15.21.19 /
You will become a famous
9.14.22.5.14.20.15.18
inventor

Fold the coded fortunes and put them in a container. Have each child pick one out and decode it. They can share their fortunes with each other.

After they get the idea, have the group use the following more complex code:

A = (4 × 1) + 3	J = 20 + (10 ÷ 5)	S = (15 ÷ 3) × 20
B = (4 × 3) − 4	K = 6 + (12 − 4)	T = (2 × 8) ÷4
C = 6 + 9 + 4	L = (2 × 9) + 2	U = 24 + (12 × 2)
D = (18 − 6) + 6	M = 47 − (10 × 3)	V = (9 + 7) + 8
E = (5 + 3) × 0	N = (52 − 47) × 5	W = 0 + (8 × 2)
F = (54 ÷ 6) + 1	O = (13 + 13) − 13	X = (24 ÷ 12) ÷ 2
G = (15 − 3) − 10	P = (9 ÷ 9) + 10	Y = (27 × 1) ÷ 3
H = (13 + 2) − 14	Q = (19 − 9) + 2	Z = (0 × 0) + 5
I = (3 × 2) + 38	R = (77 − 7) − 20	

Place this code on the board and have the children work out the numerical value of each letter. Check the results together and have them code and decode more fortunes.

HUMAN CLOCKS

MATERIALS: Chalk.

Draw a large circle on the floor. Ask the children to name the numbers on the clock. Then ask for volunteers to place themselves in the twelve positions. Begin with one person taking the twelve place, then the six, the three, and so on. When all the places are filled and the class agrees that it has been correctly done, mark the positions with chalk. The children remain in the clock positions.

Ask the other children to choose partners and decide on a time they will show on the human clock. The partners have to agree on who will be the large hand and who the small. The large hand lies down with his arms outstretched above his head, the small hand with his arms at his side. Each couple shows a time on the clock, and the teacher chooses someone to tell the time. The time is recorded on the board so other couples will not repeat it.

This can be adapted to whatever level of time telling the children can handle.

GEOMETRIC PICTURES

MATERIALS: Crayons or paint, colored paper if available, scissors, and paste.

Have the children make designs using only geometric shapes. You might limit these to circles, triangles, and rectangles (including squares) of many sizes. The shapes may be crayoned or painted or, if colored paper is available, cut out and pasted on another piece of paper.

Point out to the children that the shapes can be overlapped to make more interesting designs and pictures.

TRIANGLE DOT BOX

MATERIALS: Paper and pencil.

Illustrate on the blackboard a 5 × 5 dot arrangement (25 dots).

```
.   .   .   .   .
.   .   .   .   .
.   .   .   .   .
.   .   .   .   .
.   .   .   .   .
```

The object of the game is to form as many triangles as possible using the dots in this arrangement.

The children pair up to play against each other. The first player draws a line connecting any two dots. Then his opponent does the same. When a player forms a triangle, he puts his initials in it. Each time he forms a triangle, he gets an additional turn. The player making the most triangles wins.

HUMAN MEASURES

MATERIALS: Yardstick or ruler.

Ask the children how they could measure their classroom

using their bodies only. They will probably suggest using a foot, a hand, or their entire body. Measure the room using their suggestions. Use children of different sizes.

Ask them to make a statement about the measurement, such as "The length of the room equals 18 Alex's feet" or "15 Erica's feet." They will become aware that the measurements vary because lengths of feet differ.

Discuss with the children the need for standard unit measures. Use one, like a yardstick, to measure the room. Ask several children to take turns making the same measurement. (Check that it is done accurately.) The idea of the need for a standard will become clear when they see that the room measurements remain the same, even though different children have used the yardstick.

HIGH CARD

MATERIALS: Heavy drawing paper or tagboard, ruler, scissors, pencils.

To play this game the children first make fraction cards — good practice in itself.

Have them measure and cut seven strips, each measuring 2 × 12 inches:

The first strip or card is left as a whole and labeled 1; the second card is divided into two equal parts, each labeled ½; the third card is divided into four equal parts, each labeled ¼. Continue with the other cards, dividing them into eighths, thirds, sixths and twelfths. All cards should then be cut up into their fractional parts.

High card is played by two people. Each child shuffles his cards and places them face down before him. The card labeled 1 should be kept beside each player for reference when needed.

The first player turns over his top card. His opponent then turns over his top card. The card with the greater value takes both. If both cards have the same value, each child turns over another card. The higher card takes all. The game continues until one child is out of cards.

MATERIALS NOT USUALLY FOUND IN CLASSROOMS

A set of large arithmetic flash cards.
A pad of graph paper — just in case.

Additional materials are not needed for the activities in this chapter since the supplies suggested are standard ones found in elementary classrooms.

DESIGNS

Name Designs

MATERIALS: Unlined paper, pencils, coloring materials such as felt pens, crayons, and colored pencils.

Ask the children to fold their papers in half. Using cursive writing, they write their names so that the letters touch the fold of the paper. Either the tops or bottoms of the letters can touch the fold.

With a pencil, rub on the back of the written side, covering the entire area where the name is written.

When the paper is opened, the name will be duplicated on the other half of the paper. Darken the lines and the design becomes evident. The design can be embellished with pencil, crayon, or felt pen.

Number Designs

MATERIALS: Unlined paper, coloring materials, or paint.

Cover the entire paper with number shapes. The numbers should vary in size, go in many directions, touch each other, and overlap at some points. Color in the spaces or areas formed by the numbers, or the areas between the numbers. Outlining some numbers or parts of them enhances the effect.

Letter Designs

MATERIALS: Unlined paper, coloring materials, or paint, glue, scissors.

Follow the directions for the above number design, using the letters of the alphabet. The children might use only the letters or initials of their names. If glue and scissors are available, the children can cut out the letter shapes and arrange them in a design on a solid background.

Graph Paper Designs

MATERIALS: Graph paper, rulers, coloring materials.

Discuss with the children the pattern presented on the graph paper. Discuss the possibilities of using this pattern.

Ask them to repeat a motif in every other box, or every two boxes, or other pattern. They might accentuate existing horizontal or vertical lines to create a design.

Stencil Designs

MATERIALS: Heavy paper if possible, but not essential, scissors, unlined paper, and coloring materials.

Fold heavy paper in half. Cut out a shape on the fold. This will give a negative and positive stencil. Either the negative or positive shape can be used or they can be used together. When using the negative shape, put it on unlined paper and color in the space. When using the positive shape, place it on the paper, outline it or color along its edges with a crayon or pencil partly on the shape and partly on the paper. By varying the placement, an allover design is created.

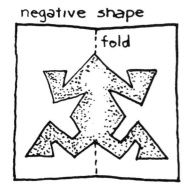

Yarn Designs

MATERIALS: Yarn, tagboard, scissors, coloring materials.

The children make several half-inch cuts around the edges of a piece of tagboard. Yarn is inserted through one cut, which holds it tightly in place. The yarn is then pulled across the tagboard and wedged in another cut, and then another and another, forming lines delineating different sized and shaped areas. The children then color in the areas between the yarn lines in various ways to make a bright design.

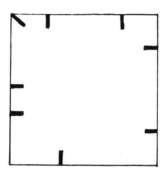 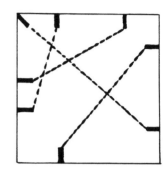

Tagboard with cuts   Yarn pulled across cuts

Smudge Designs

MATERIALS: Pastels, paper, cotton balls or tissues.

Give each child two pieces of paper. He should tear one of them into interesting shapes. He then takes a pastel and rubs some color onto a ball of cotton or a tissue. Placing one of the torn shapes firmly on the other piece of paper, he rubs the colored cotton ball or tissue along its outer edges so that the color smudges onto the underlying paper. When he lifts the torn shape, its contours will be outlined on the paper below.

The torn shapes can be placed in a variety of patterns or overlap, and other colors can be added to the cotton or tissue to create interesting effects.

Carbon Copy Designs

MATERIALS: Crayons, pencils, paper.

Fold the paper in half. Cover one half of the inside with crayon. The children then draw with pencils a picture or a design on the outer half of the crayoned side. The crayoned half acts as carbon when the pencil presses on it. The picture or design will be repeated on the clean half of the inner fold and repeated in negative form on the crayoned half.

Crayon Scratches

MATERIALS: Tagboard, index cards or other heavy paper, crayons with lots of extra black ones.

Protect the desks with newspaper or whatever is available. Cover all areas of the paper with a thick layer of crayons. Encourage the children to use many bright colors for this step. Then cover the bright colors completely with black crayon.

Tell the children to take a pointed object (paper clip, scissors, brass head, key, or other sharp instrument) and scratch a picture or a design on the black crayon. The bright colors will show through the black and make an attractive contrast.

Rubbings

MATERIALS: Coloring materials, unlined paper, objects with uneven surfaces, such as coins, keys, or paper clips. If there are trees on the playground, take a walk with the children and gather some leaves. The children can suggest other objects to work with.

Place the unlined paper over the object. Using the side of a crayon or pencil rub on the paper over the object. An impression will come through. Continue to create a design by varying the placement of the object.

Doodle Tracings

MATERIALS: Paper, coloring materials, pencils, objects that can be traced such as scissors, paper clips, ruler or other things available in the classroom.

Choose one object, place it anywhere on the paper. Trace it, move it to a new spot, and trace it again. Choose other objects and do the same thing, overlapping some areas. Cover the entire paper.

Fill in some of the spaces that have been created with color or darken the outlines in some areas. This will create an abstract doodling design.

The same thing can be done with freehand doodles.

MURALS

Easily Organized Mural

MATERIALS: Large paper for background, smaller paper for individual work, scissors, stapler or glue, coloring materials.

Have the group decide on a theme, such as a winter scene, spring garden, wild animals and their habitat, domestic animals, or dinosaurs. As the children suggest items that can be drawn to depict a particular theme, list them on the board. Ask for volunteers to draw these and cut them out. Choose a small group of children to put in the background on the large paper. When the individual items are colored and cut out, decide with the children where the best placement would be on the big background paper. Glue or staple them on. Voila— a mural complete in an hour.

For more involved suggestions, see "Do A Mural in a Day", in chapter For Courageous Substitutes, pages 36–7.

PAPER CUTTING ACTIVITIES

Paper People

MATERIALS: Heavy paper, unlined light-weight paper if available, colored paper, colored pages from magazines, scissors, and coloring materials.

Discuss with the children the fashions of the day and how they have changed, especially for boys and men. Set up some categories of clothes for different occasions, such as formal wear, beach, skiing, car racing, horseback riding, sky diving, uniforms, rain wear, and so on. The children can design clothes suitable for these categories.

The figures to be dressed should be drawn on the heavy paper and cut out. The clothing is made on light-weight paper, colored paper or magazine pages. The clothes need to be made with tabs, so they can be hung on the figures.

After the work period a fashion show can be held. The fashions should be shown in categories.

Boys who may not be interested in clothes can design cars (real or imaginative) or airplanes.

Cut-out Zoo

MATERIALS: Heavy paper, envelopes if available, scissors, coloring materials.

Elicit from the children the names of animals found in a zoo and list them on the blackboard. Tell the children they are going to make a zoo on their desks and to decide which animals they want to make.

Fold the heavy paper in half. Draw the animal so its back or head is on the fold. If envelopes are used, treat the top edge same way. When the animals are cut out, the fold must be kept in tact. This will enable the animals to stand upright.

Cut-out People

MATERIALS: Construction paper or 5 × 8 index cards, scissors, glue or staples, coloring materials.

The children decide on the members of a family. They draw each figure, color its clothes, and cut it out. Each figure will need a platform to enable it to stand.

To make the platform, cut a piece of paper 1 × 3 inches. Glue or staple the feet of the figure to this paper. Cut out a second paper 1 × 5 inches. Fold it in half. Cut a slit about an inch from the fold. Insert the first paper (containing the figure) into the slits of the partially folded platform, and the figure will stand.

Or elicit from the children names of community helpers and list them on the board. Let the children choose the helpers they want to make. Use the same materials and method described above.

In the upper grades children can create characters from incidents in history, scenes from books, and the like for original skits. Use the same materials and method as described above.

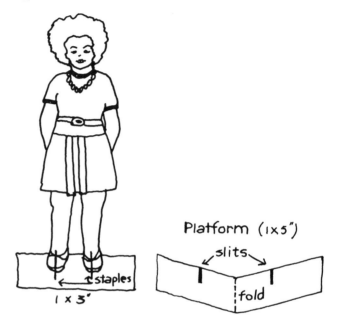

Partners or small groups can use these various kinds of figures for dramatic play.

Paper Mosaics

MATERIALS: Colored paper, background paper, scissors, glue.

The children sketch in a picture on the background paper. Then they select colored paper and cut it into narrow strips. From the strips they can cut varying sizes and shapes to fill in the picture on their background papers.

Torn Paper Pictures

MATERIALS: Background paper, colored paper, glue.

Here, the children do not draw a picture first. They build it up from torn pieces of colored paper that they glue onto the background paper. The jagged edges created by tearing make interesting effects.

MINIATURES

Miniature Scenes

MATERIALS: 3 x 5 index cards cut in half or other sturdy paper
approximately this size, pencils, coloring materials.

The children draw a scene with many details on the small
card. This forces them to do everything in miniature and
creates lovely effects. Arrange an art exhibit when all are
finished.

Miniature Designs

MATERIALS: Unlined paper, coloring materials.

Each child folds his paper into as many equal size boxes
as he thinks he can handle. In each box, he draws a separate
scene or design. The total effect created by the many miniature
designs can be exciting.

As a variation, fold paper into strips like a fan, and draw a
different design on each strip.

SKETCHING

Sketching Faces

MATERIALS: Unlined paper, pencils, charcoals, or crayons.

Before starting to work directly on the paper help the
children sense the shape of their faces and the approximate
placement of the features. Ask them to feel their own face to
visualize its basic oval shape. Have them slip their hands
down to their necks to realize the difference in width between
the face and neck. Have them observe their neighbor and
sketch his face and neck.

To develop some guide lines for placing the features of the
face, have the children observe how far down the eyes and
nose come from the top of the forehead—eyes approximately
one-third, tip of nose approximately two-thirds down. The
tip of the ear is in line with the bottom of the nose.

Have them place guide lines on the oval they have sketched.

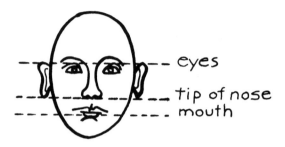

Using the guide lines, have them sketch in the features of their neighbor. They can complete their pictures with as much detail as they wish.

When all are finished, hang a portrait gallery and see if they can identify who's who.

If you are coming back a second day, ask the children to bring mirrors so they can sketch themselves.

Sketching Figures

MATERIALS: Unlined paper, pencils, coloring materials.

Ask for a volunteer to be a model. Use the model to discover the proportion of the body and develop some guide lines for sketching.

Using your hands, measure the model's face from forehead to chin. Ask the children how many of this measure will fit into the torso. They will discover approximately two. Using the same measure, see how many fit into the legs (approximately two).

For guide lines let the children start out with five equal parts—one for the head, two for the body, and two for the legs. Have them complete the figure with as much detail as they like. If they become stumped on how to draw some parts of the body, ask them to observe the model again and develop guide lines together.

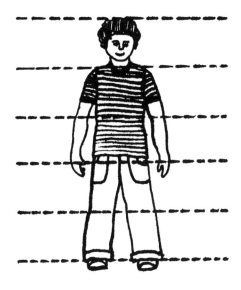

Sketching Trees

MATERIALS: Paper, pencil, charcoal, or crayon.

Have the children observe the trunk of a tree and notice the pattern made by the bark. Ask them to use this pattern to create an allover design on their papers. Do the same with the pattern of the leaves. After they have completed both design papers, let the children try to sketch the tree itself.

OPTICAL ILLUSIONS

Moving Pictures

MATERIALS: Heavy paper approximately 3 x 3 inches, stapler, scissors, pencils, coloring materials.

Have the children cut the paper to the approximate size— about five pieces per child. The children draw a figure or a simple scene on each page. Each drawing needs to be slightly different from the preceding one. For example, if a girl standing is on the first page, she should be drawn slightly bent over on the next page. Each drawing should show her bent lower than the preceding one, and on the final page she should be touching the floor. Another example is a face starting in a frown and ending in a smile on the last page. All the drawings are stapled together and then quickly flipped. This will give the illusion of movement.

Spinning Pictures

MATERIALS: Tagboard or cardboard, scissors, string, pencils or coloring materials.

Have the children cut a circular shape out of cardboard. Then they draw a picture on one side of the circle. They turn the circle over and upside down and draw a related picture. For example, a dog on one side and a dog house on the other, a cow and a field, or a butterfly and a flower. Next, attach a looped string to opposite sides of the circle.

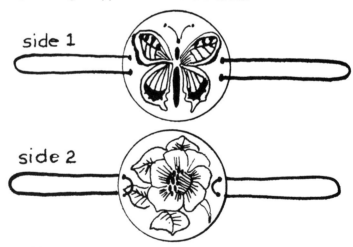

Holding the ends of both strings, twirl the circle until the strings are twisted as far as they will go. Then pull out on the strings. The picture will turn quickly and give the illusion of movement, i.e., the dog into the doghouse and the butterfly onto the flower.

HOLIDAYS

Many of the activities in this chapter are interchangeable and can be adapted for use with more than one holiday.

HALLOWEEN

Haunted Houses

MATERIALS: Paper, scissors, glue or stapler, crayons.

Discuss with the children what they think a haunted house might look like and what might be found in it. List their ideas on the board.

Next, distribute large pieces of paper and have the children draw haunted houses. In the space for the windows and doors ask them to draw surprising or scary things that might be found in a haunted house.

From other paper, cut out window shades, shutters or curtains, and a door. Glue these on the house so that they can be folded back. Behind these glued-on sections are the children's conceptions of ghosts, witches, and apparitions. Each child can then fold back his doors and shutters and show the class what is in his haunted house.

Skits

MATERIALS: None.

Divide the group into four or five committees. Designate where each group will work in the room. Give the children a time limit to work out a skit based on a Halloween theme.

As each group performs, the rest of the class is the audience.

Paper Bag Masks

MATERIALS: Paper bags, coloring materials, scissors, stapler or glue.

First, have each child put a bag over his head and mark the places for his eyes, nose, and mouth. They cut out those areas and then decorate the bag with whatever coloring materials are available. Glue or staple on colored paper as additional decorations.

Paper Plate Masks

MATERIALS: Paper plates, coloring materials, stapler, rubber bands or string.

Follow the steps for paper bag masks. Staple rubber bands to each side of the plate to fit around ears or staple on string and tie around the head.

Paper Masks

MATERIALS: Paper, coloring materials, stapler or paper clips, glue.

Each child cuts a rectangular piece of paper which will go around his head and overlap a little for fastening. The eye areas should be cut out.

On the front of his paper each child draws the face of a Halloween character. Use colored paper for decoration. The mask is fitted to each child's face and the overlap is fastened with staples or clips.

Nylon Masks

MATERIALS: Tops of nylon stockings, old make-up.

Put a nylon stocking top over each child's head and face. His features will be distorted. Use make-up to further distort the eyes, mouth, and other facial features. The children will be happy to decorate each other.

These masks can be used in children's Halloween skits or plays.

Halloween Mural

MATERIALS: Large piece of kraft paper, smaller drawing paper, crayons or other coloring materials, scissors.

Discuss with the children the kinds of things they might put in a big Halloween picture. List them on the board. Have each child decide which one he will make. When the children are finished, collect the drawings and together decide where they will be placed on the large paper.

Blackboard Art

MATERIALS: Blackboard, chalk, paper, pencils.

Decide on one Halloween theme, for example, cats or witches. Have one group work at the board drawing their ideas. The others can work on paper at their seats, while waiting for their turn.

Trick or Treat Bag

MATERIALS: Paper bags, colored paper, scissors, staplers, glue, coloring materials.

Use the colored paper to cut a strip for a handle. It can be fastened to the bag with several staples. Decorate the bag with Halloween themes.

Halloween Limericks

MATERIALS: Paper and pencils.

List with the children all the words they can think of having to do with Halloween. Briefly discuss the limerick form of verse (see language arts chapter, page 29.) and have the group make one up together. Children can then work on making up their own limericks.

Continuation Story

MATERIALS: None

Ask for a volunteer to begin a story (or do it yourself) with a Halloween theme. Each child then contributes one line orally to continue the story.

Scrambled Halloween Words

MATERIALS: Paper and pencils.

The following is a list of Halloween words. Put them on the board in scrambled form and have the children unscramble them. They may work with partners.

ghost. . . .gtsho	moon	haunted
witch. . . .tiwch	broomstick	mysterious
scary	spooky	night
owl	bewitched	bat
cat	howl	screech
goblin	Halloween	pumpkin
spirit	graveyard	

Halloween Word Game

MATERIALS: Paper and pencils.

Write the word "Halloween" on the board. Ask the children to make as many words as they can using the letters of the word. Letters may be used only as many times as they appear in the word "Halloween."

THANKSGIVING

Miniature Scene

MATERIALS: Heavy paper, coloring materials, scissors, colored paper.

Discuss with the children the origins of Thanksgiving. Have the children suggest possible scenes they can imagine. List these, for example, landing of the *Mayflower,* Indians bringing contributions to the feast, the feast itself, planting corn, or a Pilgrim village.

Each child can decide which scene he would like to make. The figures and other parts of the scene should be drawn on heavy paper, cut out, and mounted on a platform so that the figures will stand.

For the platform you will need two pieces of heavy paper, one piece 1 × 5 inches and the other 1 × 3 inches. On the smaller piece glue or staple the figure (house, tree, boat, or person). Fold the larger piece in half and cut a slit about one inch from the fold. Insert the cut-out figure into the slits and it will stand upright (see illustration on page 84).

With these figures each child can arrange a scene on his desk. They can also be used as settings for a dramatic play.

Thanksgiving Menu

MATERIALS: Paper and pencils.

Have the children make up a menu for a feast using each letter of the word "Thanksgiving" to name a food. For example, T for turkey, H for ham, A for apple and so on.

Primary children can make a realistic menu by drawing the different foods on paper, cutting them out, and arranging them on their desks before pasting them on another piece of "menu" paper.

Leaf Rubbings

MATERIALS: Leaves.

If there are trees on the school grounds, you can connect Thanksgiving with the fall season by making leaf rubbings (see Rubbings in art chapter, page 81).

CHRISTMAS

Snowflakes

MATERIALS: Lightweight paper, scissors, coloring materials.

Cut the paper into a square. Fold it in half from left to right, and then fold in half again from top to bottom. Fold from bottom left corner to upper right corner, forming a triangle. Then take the apex of the triangle and fold it down so that it extends beyond the base of the triangle. Cut off the piece which extends and snip off pieces all around the triangle including corners so that when you open out the paper it will resemble a snowflake.

These can be colored or decorated, and strung up around the room, glued to large paper for a snowflake mural, or pasted in the fold of another paper to make a greeting card.

Free-hanging Snowman

MATERIALS: Heavy paper, scissors, colored paper, coloring materials, string, glue.

Cut three circles of varying sizes for the head and large parts of the body. Hands, facial features, hat, pipe, scarf, and buttons can be cut from colored paper and glued on. If colored paper is not available, draw these parts on white paper and color it.

Punch holes in the top of each circle and pull a string through. A hat can also be hung with string so that the snowman will be mobile.

A free-hanging Santa Claus can be made in the same way.

Tiny Scenes

MATERIALS: 3 x 5 inch index cards or other paper cut small,

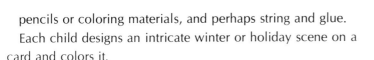
pencils or coloring materials, and perhaps string and glue.

Each child designs an intricate winter or holiday scene on a card and colors it.

If suspended with string, the scenes can be used as Christmas ornaments or as a mobile. They can also be pasted onto a larger piece of paper and used as a greeting card.

Gift Wrappings

MATERIALS: Kraft paper or newspaper, scissors, coloring materials.

Stencil Method

Create a stencil by first cutting a holiday symbol out of heavier paper. The cut-out design can be placed on the Kraft paper and coloring or tracing can be done around the edges. Repeat this all over the paper.

The cut-out form can also be used as a stencil by tracing it on the Kraft paper and filling in the empty space.

Doodle Method

Tell the children to place their pencils in the middle of the butcher paper and then look away from the paper. Ask them to move their pencils around on the paper in full swings. After a short time have them examine the design they have made and to look for areas to fill in with colors or textures. This will create an interesting wrapping.

Rubbing Method

Rubbing crayons over objects with rough, uneven surfaces gives a textured feeling to the wrapping (see Rubbings in art chapter, page 81).

VALENTINE'S DAY

Word Designs

MATERIALS: Paper, coloring materials.

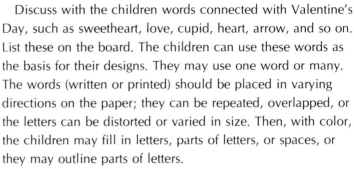

Discuss with the children words connected with Valentine's Day, such as sweetheart, love, cupid, heart, arrow, and so on. List these on the board. The children can use these words as the basis for their designs. They may use one word or many. The words (written or printed) should be placed in varying directions on the paper; they can be repeated, overlapped, or the letters can be distorted or varied in size. Then, with color, the children may fill in letters, parts of letters, or spaces, or they may outline parts of letters.

If they are to be used as cards with messages written inside, have the children work on smaller paper. Designs on large paper make a very effective mural. For this activity the children take turns writing their word.

Love Symbol Designs

MATERIALS: Paper, coloring materials.

List with the children the symbols of Valentine's Day such as hearts, arrows, cupids, and flowers.

For their own cards the children can work in the same way as for word designs above. For a mural, they can make their designs at their desks, cut them out, and then decide where to place them on a big paper.

Decorated Doilies

MATERIALS: Paper doilies, which can be purchased inexpensively in a five and ten cent store, coloring materials.

This is a simple activity enjoyed by all children. Distribute the doilies and let the children decorate them with color. The intricacy of the doily lends itself to beautiful color designs.

Love Puzzles

MATERIALS: Heavy paper, scissors, pencils, coloring materials.

Draw a fairly large heart. Write a Valentine message on it and decorate it. With pencil draw lines to create a jigsaw-type puzzle. Cut along the lines and trade puzzles with a friend.

EASTER

Easter Bunnies

MATERIALS: Paper, scissors, colored paper, staples or glue.

Take a rectangular-shaped paper and roll it into a cylinder. Staple it together. From another piece of paper cut out ears and attach them to the cylinder. The ears will look more realistic if they are creased down the center before attaching them. With colored paper add eyes, nose, mouth, eyelashes, and tail. Remind the children to use paper sculpture techniques such as fringing, accordion folding, rolling on a pencil, or other ideas they can think of to make the additions more interesting.

Spring Flowers

MATERIALS: Bring an iron from home, paper, crayons.

Fold the paper in half. Open it. On one side of the fold the children draw flowers, a single flower, or a bouquet. When finished, they refold the paper, with the flower drawing on the inside, and bring it up for ironing.

While the children are working, set up an ironing station. On a desk, near an outlet, place several layers of newspaper, a magazine, or other paper. When ironing, place a paper over the child's folded paper to prevent crayons from soiling the iron. The heat of the iron on the crayon creates an impressionistic-like flower picture.

These can be used for greeting cards or cut out and put on a class flower mural.

More Spring Flowers

MATERIALS: Paper, felt pens or black crayons, water colors.

Another technique for making spring flowers is to use felt pens and water color. The idea here is to outline the flower with a felt pen (preferably) or black crayon. Then wash in with water colors and *don't* try to keep within the lines.

Spring Murals

MATERIALS: See preceding Easter activities.

The children can create a mural using the above techniques or other simple methods. Discuss first with them the things to be included. For example, birds, butterflies, insects and bugs, flowers, trees, or grass. Have the children decide which items they're going to prepare. Have them work at their desks and cut out their finished picture. Then glue the pictures onto a larger paper.

Easter Egg Drawings

MATERIALS: Paper, coloring materials, scissors, glue or staples.

Each child needs two pieces of paper; 8½ × 11 inches is a good size. On one paper he creates an allover design. He folds the other paper in half. On the fold he draws half an oval. When he cuts it out, he will have the shape of an egg. This paper is glued or stapled over the design paper. It creates a framed Easter egg that can be used as a greeting card.

MATERIALS NOT USUALLY FOUND IN CLASSROOMS

HALLOWEEN
  Paper bags.
  Paper plates.
  Tops of nylon stockings.
  Old make-up.
CHRISTMAS
  Large spool of thread or string.
VALENTINE'S DAY
  Doilies.
EASTER
  Iron.
  Newspaper.

Rainy Days

Any of the games of other countries given in the Social Studies Chapter would work very well here (see pages 53–5).

CIRCUS TIME

MATERIALS: Marching or circus music record, if possible.

Discuss with the children the many kinds of acts that are presented in a circus, for example, animal training, clowns, tightrope acts, trapeze stunts, bareback riding, and so on. List these on the board. Then choose a master of ceremonies (an outgoing, verbal child).

It's important to discuss each of the acts listed so that the children can develop ideas of how each performer walks, what movements he uses in his act, the expression of his body and his face—in other words, what makes the "character" of the performer.

Ask for volunteers to work out the acts. Put the names of the volunteers next to the act written on the board. Allow time to practice. Decide how to arrange the room to provide a performing area.

When the children are ready, play the music and have a circus parade. The master of ceremonies acts as a barker arousing the enthusiasm of the crowd. After the parade, he calls each act separately into the arena while the other children are the audience.

MAKING YOUR OWN ORCHESTRA

MATERIALS: A tape recorder if possible. Look around for anything that can be used to make a rhythmic sound, for example: rubber bands for twanging, pencils and rulers for tapping, jars that can be filled with water to different levels for tapping, containers that can be partly filled with objects for rattling, combs to be hummed on or snapped, or the children for snapping or tapping fingers, stamping feet, humming, or whistling.

Before you begin this activity discuss with the children how an orchestra performs together and how a conductor uses signals to direct. Point out how important it is for each musician to watch the conductor and to listen to one another. The children will respond to the idea that they are in a recording studio and the need for no unnecessary noises. If you can record their performance on a tape, so much the better.

Begin with volunteers. Have each child decide which sound he wants to make. Those making the same sound form a group. Allow each group to work separately and to create its own rhythm.

Select a conductor. The orchestra is assembled so that each sound group is seated together. The conductor points his baton (ruler) to a section of the orchestra. It begins its rhythm. The children repeat their sound until it is clearly established. Then the conductor points to another group to join in. The idea is

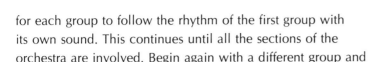

for each group to follow the rhythm of the first group with its own sound. This continues until all the sections of the orchestra are involved. Begin again with a different group and its own rhythm.

Another way to handle the orchestra activity is to have groups work out individual performances. In this case, groups can be composed of different "instruments" which the children can use to develop complementary rhythms. Each group then performs separately for the entire class.

After trying these first two approaches, the class may be ready to try some improvisation. The conductor chooses one person to begin. When his rhythm is established, the conductor points to someone else to come in and complement what is already started. Continue until everyone is involved.

ROCK AND ROLL SHOWCASE

MATERIALS: A few rock and roll records.

Designate two places in the room as showcase areas and ask for volunteers to dance in them. Select a few to begin. The others will watch while they dance. You may choose other children who want to dance to exchange places with the showcase dancers at any time.

If most of the class becomes interested, you might allow all the children to dance at once. Those who want to "showcase" can raise their hands. You tap a dancer in the showcase area to exchange places.

WHO'S MISSING?

MATERIALS: None.

The child who is IT leaves the room. Another person then either hides or leaves the room being careful not to be seen by IT. IT is called back and tries to figure out who is missing.

KING AND QUEEN

MATERIALS: Two board erasers.

Choose a king and a queen. A board eraser is placed on each head as a crown. The king stands at one end of the room and the queen at the other. At a given signal they start walking toward each other. The object of the game is for the king and queen to tag each other without losing their crowns. If a crown falls off, the player is eliminated, and someone else takes over. The winner is the one who tags the other and keeps the crown on his own head.

CHIEF

MATERIALS: None.

The children form a circle. One person is chosen to be IT and goes out of the room. Choose a chief from the remaining children. At a signal the chief begins a movement or makes a sound. All the other children follow his lead. The child who is IT is called back into the room and goes into the center of the circle. Now he must figure out who the chief is. The object of the game is for the chief to lead the class in changing movements and not be discovered by IT.

Usually IT has three guesses. If the chief is identified, he becomes IT and goes out of the room and another chief is chosen.

HAND TRACING RELAY

MATERIALS: Blackboard and chalk.

Divide the class into two teams. Each lines up facing the blackboard. At a signal the first child on each team walks up to the board and places his hand on it. With chalk he traces the outline of his hand, delineating all of the fingers. When finished, he sits down at his seat and the next child comes up. The first team to finish with everyone seated is the winner.

GOSSIP

MATERIALS: None.

Divide the class into two groups. Each group stands in a line shoulder to shoulder. The teacher whispers a simple message into the ear of the first person in each line. That person quickly whispers the message to the next person in line. The message is passed down the line until the last person receives it.

The object is to pass the message as quickly and accurately as possible. The line that finishes first waits for the other to finish. Then, the last person receiving the message in each line tells it to the class. The children will enjoy seeing how distorted it has become.

The first person in each line now goes to the end and another message is given. After playing a couple of times, let a child make up the message.

SEVEN UP

MATERIALS: None.

Choose seven children to go up to the front of the room. The first one chosen is the captain.

The captain gives the command to the seated children, "Heads down, thumbs up." The children put their heads down on the desk, hiding their eyes, and put one thumb up.

The seven standing children tiptoe around the room. Each one taps the thumb of one child. As soon as a child feels his thumb touched, he puts it down still keeping his eyes hidden.

After the seven have finished they go back to the front of the room. The captain now calls, "Seven up." The seven children whose thumbs have been tapped stand up. The captain asks each one in turn, "Who tapped you?" If he guesses correctly, he takes the place of the child standing in front. After all have had a chance to guess, the children up front who were not identified tell who they tapped and then the game begins again.

For a variation the child tapping a thumb disguises his voice and says, "I choose you." The rest of the game proceeds as above.

BIRD, BEAST, FISH

MATERIALS: A ball made out of crushed paper.

Choose one girl or boy to come to the front of the room. He throws a ball of crushed paper to a child in the room. As soon as the ball leaves his hand, he calls one of the three categories, *bird, beast,* or *fish* and counts to ten. Before the count reaches ten, the child who catches the ball must name a creature fitting the category. If he succeeds, he gets to throw the ball. If not, the child in front throws again.

The game can also be played with the categories of *animal, vegetable* or *mineral.*

MATERIALS NOT USUALLY FOUND IN CLASSROOMS

CIRCUS TIME

March or circus music record.

ROCK AND ROLL SHOWCASE

A few rock and roll records.

children talk about substitutes

The following comments about substitute teachers were written anonymously by children in the middle and upper elementary grades in the Los Angeles City School System. They probably are representative of the feelings of children everywhere.

They're too bossy. They always say your name wrong. They don't know me, and I don't know them.

Dear Mrs. Sub,
From my advice to you I think a sub should come prepared, make things fun, not the old stuff like write your spelling words 12 times and underline the silent letters. We are used to that. I think you will be liked more if you try to make things interesting.

Sincerely,
A child

I think the first day the substitute should bring something fun to do just so that the kids will know she's not all that bad.

She shouldn't talk too much so the children could get their work done.

Don't stay on regular schedule 'cause that's boring. Really, you're something special, and if you come with books like English and math your're not special anymore.

Have a good sense of humor.

I like the kind that give you all play and no work, but I never had a sub who did that.

A sub should be a person with NO temper. She shouldn't yell and scream like regular teachers sometimes do. We need a break, too, sometimes.

I have had many subs in my life. I like seeing new ladies. I like to see if they're nice or mean. It's better than the same teacher all the time.

We once had a sub that was pregnant and she always was nervous, and we had a sweet sub that had a low voice and didn't yell.

Once I had a substitute in third grade and she brought a little puppet to show and she did art.

Subs, even the nicest ones, make your regular teacher look good because your regular teacher knows your name.

A lot of substitutes explain the math to us and mix me up because they explain it differently.

I think a substitute is nice when she walks in and says, "Hi" and says her name.

When the sub is coming, the teacher puts more work on the schedule than usual and then the sub comes and she follows it inch by inch. She just keeps piling on the work.

They don't know what's going on and cause confusion. But so that they can have time to figure things out, they give you extra P. E. or films or art.

They get everything mixed up. They do stuff you already know. When they get mad, they blow up a lot more than regular teachers. They slam books down, they scream loud to drive you mad. Then the class starts to cut up more.

I think most subs are pretty nice because they can give you chances because they don't know what kind of reputation you already have.

All they do is follow the plan book and if they don't know how to do the subject she will ask the class. Then all the children start to argue. The teacher gets all mad and people have to write.

They yell a lot at you because you're not as well-disciplined as her last class.

I don't like subs because I try to take advantage of them.

I like to have subs because sometimes I like to have a change because you get bored of doing the same thing every day.

Some have you write your name on a card, and I can understand that, but when they make you wear it outside—that's ridiculous.

I think a substitute should not be too strict or mean, but not too nice to let the whole room turn into a madhouse, even though I like them that way.

I think a sub should be as nice as possible and shouldn't bawl out one child in front of the class.

She should listen to questions.

I like subs because they bring things that I have never heard of. They teach us to make things like witches and ghosts for Halloween and to fold paper into flowers. They read funny stories.

I think that the substitute should treat the children just like they were their own class.

If she is there for one day, she should try and control them as best as she can.

She could like tell jokes or laugh. That's the best way to be a good sub.

Try not to shout at kids, even if they do something terrible. Just keep smiling (maybe). Another thing is to always keep them busy. Don't give them spelling or language assignments. Give them fun things to do.

When a sub is your teacher, you would think that the day will be a bore, but if the substitute comes in prepared with different games and puzzles or art projects the day will be better for everyone.

They brag about their other students and expect you to listen.

Sometimes we do fun things that we don't normally do. Sometimes they're mean and follow everything in the plan book word for word and it seems like a normal day and it gets boring.

In the morning for substitutes it is terrible! It seems everyone says, "Boo, boo, boo." If you start out telling jokes that would do. First you must coax them into working by putting fun things ahead which makes them excited. Perhaps if they're excited, they could work faster. Put fun things in instead of boring things. Boring things don't let children learn.

She should not have an assignment that you think will never end.

I don't like them because they don't know your name and they might call you red hair or black hair kid.

I don't like substitute teachers because they do not know what you are doing and they do it differently than your teacher shows you how.

I think a sub shouldn't follow the teacher's exact words. I think you should make something out of it. She shouldn't treat you like you're at an obedience school.

He or she can be nice or mean, but either way everyone gets excited by the thought that it is going to be a different kind of day.

I do not like subs because I am used to my regular teacher.

I think a good teacher would say to the class, "My name

is ____. If you're good in the morning we will have individual projects."

The good thing about a sub is that you get a lot of talk, not work. A lot of games too. But some subs are grumpy. I remember a sub I had that was a constant grumble. No smile or anything. Nothing but work.

They get confused and ask some stupid kid, who doesn't know what they're talking about, something that doesn't really matter at all.

The ones who were nice did art projects with us. The ones who were mean just grouched all day at us.

I don't like the old crabby ones. They sound like an injured old crow. The young ones are nice because they can remember my name.

If a substitute teacher, on her first job, asked me for advice, I would tell her: don't be too strict, don't be afraid to ask questions, don't feel embarrassed and don't be stiff!

It really doesn't matter — it's a teacher.